How to Help Your Preschooler

Learn... More... Faster... & Better

HOW TO HELP YOUR
LEARN... MORE...

PRESCHOOLER
FASTER... & BETTER

David Melton

David McKay Company, Inc. / New York

To Glenn J. Doman

*—Who, in all probability, knows more about the
neurological development of children than anyone else in
the world . . . better still, he knows the right things.
—Whose vast respect for the amazing learning potentials
of young children and the innate teaching abilities of
mothers has created one of the gentlest revolutions the
world has ever known.*

Library of Congress Cataloging in Publication Data

Melton, David.
    How to help your preschooler learn . . . more . . . faster . . . &
better.

    Includes bibliographical references and index.
    1. Education, Preschool. 2. Domestic education.
3. Educational acceleration. 4. Mentally handicapped
children—Education. I. Title.
LB1140.2.M445   372.21   76-25423
ISBN 0-679-50614-4
ISBN 0-679-50633-0 pbk.

MANUFACTURED IN THE UNITED STATES OF AMERICA

Editor, Marion Boike

Contents

Introduction

The secret is out again.

I've just read the headline in the *Philadelphia Inquirer,* "Even Toddlers Are Now Playing Violin and Piano." Such a headline provides a fitting prologue for David Melton's book, *How to Help Your Preschooler Learn . . . More . . . Faster . . . & Better.*

Beginning with *How to Teach Your Baby to Read* by Glenn Doman, written in 1962, the secret, known before to an enlightened few, that tiny children have an immeasurable ability to learn has created "The Gentle Revolution," which was, in fact, the book's subtitle. Since that time, this secret has made headlines with increasing frequency. I guess that means it is not really a secret anymore, doesn't it?

From time to time we have all come into contact with or read stories about an unusual child with some extraordinary ability in music, math, languages or art. Until recently, however, everyone assumed that such children have had some inborn talent. Yet, when we study the early environments of such children, we find that there has always been a relative or a friend with a special interest in the same area in which the child has developed his or her own superior ability.

The findings are too consistent and significant to blame coincidence in each of the many cases. From this data we can learn that such children do not represent some isolated phenomena, but in fact demonstrate what any child could learn if given the opportunity and encouragement to do so. Better still, a growing number of people are becoming convinced that *all* children have the potential to develop *all* of the abilities which in the past have occurred as single talents recognized in a tiny number of children.

The profound influence of the environment on a child

seems to me nowhere more clearly illustrated than in the occasional child who has been discovered living in the wild. In these cases the early learning has been profound, and when tested, irreversible. Such children have adapted to the behavior and communication patterns of whatever animals have fostered them, and this early learning has been so deeply ingrained that none of them have ever successfully readjusted later in their lives to human society.

In one of my favorite songs from the Broadway musical *South Pacific,* the lyricist, Oscar Hammerstein II, wrote quite aptly and quite correctly, "You've got to be taught before it's too late, before you are six or seven or eight. . . ." Truer words have never been written or sung. While Mr. Hammerstein stresses in his song that prejudices must be taught at very early ages, scientists are now finding that young children can learn all kinds of information easier and better than can older ones.

I have only one reservation with Mr. Hammerstein's conclusion, which says, "You've got to be carefully taught." Happily, that might be true for older people who learn very slowly, but it certainly isn't so for children before they are "six or seven or eight." Then they learn so quickly and easily that it is a constant marvel to the adults around them.

In children's early years we do not really teach them anything in formal organized classroom situations. And while most children are carefully cared for, there is nothing careful or very organized about the stimulation they receive there. Children are keen observers of their surroundings and quickly begin to mimic what they see and hear. What is seen and heard by most children in the mundane routine of family life is picked up so quickly that it seems to be absorbed by osmosis. The unfortunate fact is that this average stimulation is enough for children to develop average abilities. But what is so good about average, when children are capable of so much more? What's wrong with superior?

With the growing recognition that children can learn so easily, there are an increasing number of mothers across the country who have earned the title, in my respect, of "professional mothers." They have devoted themselves to providing their children with an enriched variety of opportunities to learn. These mothers are not only interested in the skills which their children develop, but also in the less tangible, but very gratifying, self-confidence, curiosity, and independence which results from their children's further developed capabilities.

In this book, David Melton not only shares the secret of young children's amazing abilities to learn but he also provides very helpful guidelines for parents, who aspire to be "professionals," in providing their preschoolers the opportunities to *"learn . . . more . . . faster . . . & better."*

Not only is teaching your child the most exciting game in town but it is one in which everyone who plays can be a winner.

Gretchen Kerr

Director, The Children's Clinic
The Institutes for the Achievement of Human Potential
Philadelphia, Pennsylvania

Although the Day Is Not Mine to Give,
I'll Show You the Morning Sun

My child, my child,
your days of childhood are quickly spent.
As the season passes,
I wonder why it hurries so.

I hope that in these years,
I have attended to more
than skinned knees and cut fingers.
I hope that somewhere in the everyday,
that I have not overlooked
the needs of your heart,
and the growth of your spirit.
I hope that somewhere in the while,
there was enough worth the while.

And if there was not . . .
and if there was not . . .
and if there was not . . .
I don't know now
how I can make it up to you.

—DAVID MELTON
I'll Show You the Morning Sun
Stanyan-Random House
Copyright © 1971

How to Help Your Preschooler
Learn... More... Faster... & Better

Chapter 1

What Is Your Preschooler Learning Today? What Did He Learn Yesterday? What Will He Learn Tomorrow?

Three Important Questions

Has your five-year-old recently read a good novel?

Does your four-year-old solve algebraic equations?

Has your three-year-old painted a masterpiece?

Is your two-year-old a student of geography?

Can your one-year-old swim?

If your child isn't doing these things or can't do these things it may not be your child's fault. He or she can probably do *all* of these things if you take only a few minutes out of your day to teach him or her how.

The fact is, very young children have the ability to learn *anything* you care to teach them.

Within these pages we will explore not only *how* young children can be taught, but we will discover *why* they are such eager learners. Better still, ways will be presented by which you can improve your child's development and even *grow* his brain. If you find the idea of growing your child's brain exciting, then you will probably enjoy reading this information as much as I have enjoyed reporting it.

I prefer to say that I am reporting this material, because these recent findings are not my insights; they are drawn from literally all parts of the world and from many fields of science. I never actively searched for this information—it seemed to drift toward me in a series of coincidences and push me with such force that I was compelled to place it in chapters and label it as a book.

The first coincidence certainly didn't seem to be fortuitous. In fact, at the time, it appeared as a tragedy, and everytime I think of how very close it came to remaining a tragedy, I break out in a cold sweat and a sudden fever invades my body.

Not long after our son was born, Nancy and I discovered that he was not developing as he should. He was slow to roll over and to sit alone. He didn't crawl properly and he didn't creep on his hands and knees. Nancy took him to a number of pediatricians only to be told repeatedly that nothing could be done to speed his development. We were told to be patient and that in time he would most likely do all the things expected of a child his age. So we waited and we watched. We saw other children growing and learning at acceptable rates while Todd developed in slow motion.

When Todd was five years old, we took him to a regional diagnostic center. After he was given a battery of tests, we were informed that he was a "slow learner," "mentally retarded," and perhaps mildly "cerebral palsied." The psychologists and the doctors said that our son might never read above a preprimer level and it was doubtful that he would advance beyond a third grade academic level. If that prognosis didn't have tragic overtones, I don't know what has.

When we asked how his condition could be improved, we were told that we should accept our boy's limitations and stop hoping that he would ever be like "normal" children.

Because my wife and I were young and because we were

both energetic and stubborn, we refused to accept that advice. As Nancy said, for five years she had been right in her assessment that Todd was not developing properly and the pediatricians had been wrong in their predictions that time would cure all ills. That day at the diagnostic clinic nothing had changed except the opinions of the professionals. Nancy was determined that those opinions would have to change again. She was determined to find a way to make Todd better. In fact, she was determined to do more than that. She wanted to make him well. Of course she didn't know how to perform that neat trick of magic. It was the elusiveness of those "hows" that gave her sleepless nights and days of anguish.

Her search led us from Kansas City to Philadelphia and The Institutes for the Achievement of Human Potential. There Todd was diagnosed as being brain-injured. Intensive programs of sensory therapy were prescribed which could be administered by us in our own home. Within three months we saw his abilities begin to improve, and after eighteen months he had progressed sufficiently to attend a regular school. Today Todd is a senior in high school and doing very well. And the goals for normality that we had set for him are being achieved.

It is not my purpose to relate our story or to tell of the problems of having a brain-injured child; I have done this already in two other books—in *Todd* (the story of those years), and in *When Children Need Help* (an exploration of the problems confronting parents in obtaining educational and medical help for their brain-injured children).

However, during the course of making Todd well and writing these books, I had the opportunity to work with Glenn Doman, the director of The Institutes. Through him, I became aware that not only is it possible to alter the abilities of brain-injured children, but by utilizing many of these methods with "average" or "superior" children during their early years, parents can accelerate their youngster's development.

And through Doman, I became aware of his work and the work of numerous researchers on national and international scenes. Their findings have broadened the world's knowledge concerning the abilities and potentials of very young children.

The three most important questions the parent of a preschooler can ask are:
- What did my child learn yesterday?
- What is he learning today?
- What will he learn tomorrow?

There is little one can do or undo about yesterdays. They are gone, gone, gone.

However, today is up for grabs. It's here and it's now. It's course can be altered.

And tomorrow? Tomorrow and all the other tomorrows in your child's early years can either be utilized or they can be wasted. The choice is yours.

If you are the parent of a preschooler, I hope this book excites your imagination and directs you into positive actions that offer your child every opportunity to learn.

If you are not the parent of a preschooler, I hope as soon as you finish reading this book, that you give it to a parent who is.

Chapter 2

A Time to Learn or a Time to Wait?

Your Child from Birth to Six

Learning is the greatest adventure in life. Learning is desirable, vital, unavoidable and, above all, life's greatest and most stimulating game. The child believes this and will always believe this—unless we persuade him that it isn't true.

—GLENN DOMAN
How to Teach Your Baby to Read[1]

In recent years there has been a lot of talk about the astonishing learning capacity of children who are younger than five years of age. When most people heard of a four-year-old or a three-year-old who could read, they would think, "Isn't that cute!" or "What on earth would a four-year-old child want to read?" or "That kid must be some kind of a freak!" However, since the advent of *Sesame Street* we either have to conclude that there are a lot of freak kids in this country or that we were wrong, and that, indeed, three- and four-year-olds not only learn to read, but they think it is fun. In fact, it appears that children under five years of age think learning how to do most anything is fun. They enjoy learning. They think it is easy.

Perhaps it has been difficult for us to believe that children can learn so effortlessly because of the many preconceived notions we have perpetrated about them. In the past, we have been told that children are nothing but little mimics who copy adults—"monkey see, monkey do" if you please. And we have made a practice of keeping them in their place. "Children should be seen, not heard." Of course, we have allowed them to be seen because they are so cute in their clumsiness and they smile well.

If, in the past, parents have viewed the abilities and the potentials of small children through dark, clouded glasses, it is not their fault. The educators and philosophers, proclaiming to know all about such things, have advised parents into numbness.

Repeatedly, the professionals told us that children have little heads and little thoughts. They said that children have short bodies and even shorter attention spans. And they told us, that since learning is a very serious business, academic instruction should not be dispersed by ordinary parents.

They warned us that teaching little children to count on more than ten fingers or toes, or undertaking to teach them to read was a crime against nature, and some even maintained that such actions were sins against God. (If God wanted little children to count beyond ten He would have given them more fingers and toes; if He wanted them to read, children would have been born with books in their hands.)

When parents ventured to ask *who* determined such things, the professionals quoted Rousseau, Gesell and Piaget with such reverence that one might suspect that these men must have descended from Mount Olympus.

If we questioned *what* these men had said, we were told that in the eighteenth century, the French philosopher J.J. Rousseau postulated that children were inherently good, and that they developed through a series of "internally regulated" stages. Society, he believed, was basically evil, and had little positive effect upon a child's intellectual growth patterns. Therefore, Rousseau maintained that the child's environment should remain as unstructured as possible to allow him to develop as his genetic nature had predetermined.[2] In other words, he proposed, if a child is ready to learn, he will learn, and if he isn't, he won't.

In the 1930's, Arnold Gesell's theory of maturation, reiterating many of Rousseau's beliefs, acquired considerable vogue among educators, philosophers, and even the lay public. Concluding that children develop by an "internal ripening" process, Gesell proposed that "parental expectations, demands, limitations and controls were unnecessary and could impair the parent-child relationship (Gesell and Ilg, 1943)."[3]

In essence, Gesell's theory of maturation might compare a child's levels of development to the blooming of a flower. At predetermined times, leaves will sprout on the stem, a bud will appear, then petals will form and begin to open. All of these stages will occur in proper sequence if the environment doesn't hinder them in some way.

As educators embraced Gesell's theories, they invented flowerlike terms to label children's maturational speeds. If a child matured faster than other youngsters he was called "a quick starter." If he developed at a slower rate than most children, he was considered "a late bloomer." It was all very lovely, but parents found it difficult to understand if they were preparing their children for school or a greenhouse.

During the last thirty years a Swiss psychologist, Jean Piaget, placing emphasis on concrete and abstract learning processes, researched and labeled the stages of childhood development. Piaget proposes that the environment *may* affect the amount of information a child will absorb within the levels of development through what he calls "self-regulation."[4]

Although the theories of Rousseau, Gesell and Piaget vary in degrees and labels and time frames, their conclusions that children develop through predetermined stages of development certainly coincide. All three advocated that *Little Bo Peep* philosophy—leave them alone and they'll grow up, wagging their predetermined stages behind them.

In the brevity of presenting the theories of Rousseau, Gesell and Piaget, it may appear that I have made light of their work. That is not my intention. I admire Rousseau's concern for the welfare of children. Gesell was a dedicated researcher. His emphasis on the nurturing of children's creative abilities offers many insights. In a later chapter, without hesitation, I quote Gesell on this subject. And few would argue with Piaget's designations of concrete and abstract learning processes in children's cognitive development. However, these men's conclusions, purporting that environment cannot significantly affect, alter, enhance, or accelerate the abilities of young children, must certainly be disputed in the light of more recent scientific research.

When They Are Ready, They Will Automatically Learn, and Other Nonesuch Stories

While the professionals stressed the predetermined levels of childhood development, most parents tried to do as they were advised and not disturb the growth patterns of their "budding flowers." But there were others who either didn't know the rules or didn't care, who enriched their children's home environments, teaching their little tulips to add, subtract, multiply, and, God forbid, some even taught them how to divide.

And some parents went so far as to teach their preschoolers to *read!* Gadzooks!

While the professionals stressed that teaching children reading and writing and mathematical concepts was an extremely difficult and time-consuming ordeal, many parents found just the opposite to be true: teaching a child these things was quite easy and required very little time.

While the professionals predicted that children who learned such things in their early years would become psychological monsters, parents saw the contrary: the more the child learned, the better adjusted he became.

Finally the professionals unleashed their last and most devastating threat, "If you teach your child to read and write and solve mathematical problems, when he gets to school, he is going to be BORED!"

Some parents were frightened by this warning and stopped teaching their children.

But others were less intimidated and said, "Now, wait a minute. Are you saying, if a child can read and write and solve mathematical problems that when he comes to school he is going to be bored?"

"Exactly!" they answered.

"Well, what do you intend to teach them at school?" these parents inquired.

"We are going to teach them reading and writing and mathematics."

"But isn't it an advantage to already be able to do these things?"

"Of course not," they answered. "If children already do these things, they have to sit and wait while we teach the others."

"Are you saying, while the other children are learning to read that those who already can read are going to be told to sit quietly and wait?"

"Of course," they answered. "Now you understand."

These parents looked straight at the professionals and replied, "That's the biggest piece of nonsense we've ever heard. If you allow children who can read and write to sit idle for days on end, how can you claim to be educators?"

"But it screws up the system!" the professionals screamed at the top of their intellectual voices.

"*Now* we understand," these parents answered. "You are so concerned with maintaining the system that you would allow bright and eager boys and girls to sit on the sidelines. That can't be called teaching, can it? Obviously, the problem is not in the children; the problem lies in preserving the system."

"But you *don't* understand. . . ."

As absurd as these conversations sound, I assure you, they have been repeated thousands and thousands of times, and although there is an enormous amount of data proving that very young children can and do learn to read with great ease, many of these ridiculous dialogues continue.

The stage was being set for a revolution in theory and in attitudes. That revolution was not long in coming.

The Gentle Revolution

In 1963, Glenn Doman's article, "You Can Teach Your Baby to Read," was printed in *Ladies' Home Journal,* and the following year, his book *How to Teach Your Baby to Read* was published.

When the book appeared on the market, many thought the idea was quaint and that Mr. Doman was joshing—that he really didn't mean *baby.* But, in fact, he *did mean baby.*

Most educators thought it was a terrible book—a missile from the enemy's camp—and they would have loved to burn both the book and Mr. Doman at the stake. However, mothers bought the book by the thousands and began to teach their babies to read by the thousands.

The subtitle of *How to Teach Your Baby to Read* is "The Gentle Revolution." Without bombs bursting in air that revolution has taken place and the world has begun to look at very young children with new respect.

In essence, Mr. Doman proposes that very young children are linguistic geniuses and that they will learn almost anything at an early age if it is presented to them in a clear, informative way.

For instance, all mothers teach their babies to hear and speak a foreign language since no baby born in the United States is born understanding English, just as no baby born in Spain understands Spanish—in Germany, German, in Portugal, Portuguese, etc. Mothers teach their children a language by speaking that language to them. And they can just as easily teach their children to read. Babies have an insatiable urge to learn, and unless they are physically impaired, they will learn at fantastic rates of speed.

Doman came to these conclusions through an extremely interesting set of circumstances. As director of The Institutes for the Achievement of Human Potential he was chiefly responsible for innovative methods of therapy designed to accelerate the abilities of brain-injured children. The goals Doman and his staff set for these children were truly revolutionary—the goal for each child was to make him completely well. A staggering idea indeed since it was considered impossible by both the medical and educational establishments.

Before Doman, it was considered that these children should be carted off to institutions where they would be out of sight of their distressed parents and warehoused with other kids like themselves. It was thought that if these children's conditions required any therapy at all this therapy should minimize the regression of their abilities. In other words, if one of these kid's muscles were tightening, the therapist would set up exercises to try to halt further atrophy. Such a treatment could be likened to a doctor giving a patient medicine to stop the cold from getting worse but giving him nothing to make him well. The thought of *improving* the conditions of these children was nothing short of heresy, and the idea that their mental capacities could be increased was considered unreasonable, wishful hoping, and even witchcraft. Obviously, those conventional beliefs were medically unsound and both psychologically and physically damaging to these children. But for want of a better reason, they were maintained because they were conventional. It was, and in many places today still is, a great tragedy.

However, Doman decided to challenge those conventions, and he assembled a staff of the brightest people he could find from the fields of medicine, education, physical therapy, etc., and set out to discover ways to make these children well. They designed methods of therapy which were performed with frequency, intensity, and duration, and some of their patients' conditions began to improve. In fact, some of these children became so much like "normal" children that they entered regular school with regular kids and no one at the school had the slightest idea that they had ever been brain-injured or labeled as "mentally retarded," "cerebral palsied," or "learning disabled."

In short order, Glenn Doman, The Institutes, and their methods became the subject of magazine articles and news stories which made them both world famous and highly controversial. No one in the history of the world has ever rocked the boat of the status quo without being confronted with fists of rage and professional skepticism.

During that time something amazing happened. The parents of one of the brain-injured children who was on the program mentioned to Doman that their son, Tommy, could read. At first, Doman thought they were exaggerating the boy's accomplishment and that he was, in all probability, able to read a word or two, or that the parents only *thought* he was reading. However at the parents' insistence, Doman watched as the five-year-old child opened a magazine and commenced to read. This would have been a feat worth watching if Tommy had been a regular kid, but it was truly astonishing to see a brain-injured boy do it.

After witnessing this scene, Doman could have arrived at several conclusions. One, that Tommy was a freak of nature and therefore, unique. Two, that he had really been a genius all along, posing as a brain-injured kid. Or, three, that if Tommy could do it, then all brain-injured children could learn to read if someone would take the time to show them how. And then, with a brilliant hypothesis, Doman projected the theory one step further—if brain-injured children could be taught to read, then well children could learn.

Soon Doman had all of The Institutes' patients on reading programs and he discovered another astonishing fact—the younger the child, the easier he could learn to read and the better reader he became. Doman realized that because of the rate of early brain growth, five-year-olds could learn faster than six-year-olds; that four-year-olds could learn faster than five-years-olds; and that two-year-olds could beat them all hands down.

Since Doman is a physical therapist and not one of their ilk, the educators cried, "Unfair!" But mothers accepted Doman's conclusions on face value. Now that many educators have come to the same conclusions, they quickly purport that after years of study and analysis *they* have come, not to Doman's conclusions, but to their *own*. Perhaps such actions verify what a *gentle* revolution Doman's has been. The truth is that eventually they *had* to come to these conclusions because Doman is right. After teachers saw so many children coming to school who could already read, they had to at least admit that children younger than five years of age could, indeed, learn to read.

Just as quickly, Doman came to another important conclusion about young children's abilities to learn—not only can they learn to speak and read a language, but they can learn to do *anything* if they are given the opportunity.

The Early Learning Bandwagon

Shortly after the publication of Glenn Doman's book, a rash of magazine articles and books hit the stores telling about this newfound insight into the development of children. And a new trend was struck. Doman had broken the ice of the mass media. Contrary to their claims, most publishers are not the champions of new ideas and innovations. However, when one publisher finds success with a book dealing with a new idea or subject, a raft of others shower the stores with the speed of summer lightning, and frequently their titles are so similar to the original book that the shopper has difficulty telling one from the other. Be that as it may, the idea caught on and everyone began talking about the amazing learning capacities of small children.

In the article, "7,000,000 Children Can't Be Wrong," Gerald S. Lesser, chairman of the board of advisers of Children's Television Workshop, said during an interview: "Children under five years old can learn much more and much faster

than most people think. This is one of the most important
lessons of the television program *Sesame Street.* . . . When
we began, we discovered that we were constantly undere-
stimating the children's ability to learn. . . ." For instance,
Lesser explains that when they started out with a simple test
for classification, they didn't know whether children would
be able to differentiate three triangles from a circle. But the
kids understood immediately, not only the forms, but sizes
and colors too.[2]

In his book *Stability & Change in Human Characteristics,*
Dr. Benjamin S. Bloom of the University of Chicago,
stresses: ". . . by four years of age, as much as 50% of a
person's intelligence is highly flexible, . . . but after that the
chances of raising a child's intelligence diminish, and more
and more powerful forces are required to produce a given
amount of change."[3]

"The child's intelligence grows as much during his first
four years of life as it will grow in the next thirteen," writes
Maya Pines in an article adapted from her book *Revolution
in Learning.* "At two or three years of age, he can learn any
language, perhaps even several languages, more easily than
any adult. During this period of extra-rapid growth, the
environment exerts its most powerful effect. . . . Unfortunately, adults often stifle these talents instead of developing
them."[4]

Such findings were not limited to the United States. In
Italy, Maria Montessori had reached many of these conclusions. Nor were the findings limited to academic studies; they
also contained possibilities for political application. Adolf
Hitler proposed that if a child were fully indoctrinated with
Nazi propaganda during the first six years of his life, he
would be a willing soldier for the rest of his days. Obviously,
the Russian and the Chinese caught onto that idea quickly
enough.

And in Japan there is Shinishi Suzuki, a man who has
opened a whole world of music to young children. Suzuki
is the son of the founder of the Suzuki Violin Factory

which, by the time Shinishi was born, was the largest in the world. As a child, Suzuki was only casually interested in the instrument—no more seriously than any shoemaker's son might regard shoes. However, later he became awe-stricken by the beautiful sounds. Borrowing a violin from the factory, he laboriously taught himself to play a Haydn minuet by listening to a record and reproducing the composition, note by note. From that moment on, he was "hooked" on the violin.

Suzuki never intended to be a teacher of the violin, but a situation occurred which afforded him great insight. As a young man he studied in Germany and had great difficulty learning the language—a predicament both troublesome and annoying. He noticed, however, that young children had little trouble learning the language, while he, a grown man, was stumbling with nouns and verbs and mouth-twisting guttural sounds. A man of lesser mind might have said, "Damn!" and walked away. But Suzuki knew he had to find an answer for this phenomenon. And find it he did.

Suzuki deduced that before the age of six, children are linguistic geniuses, and then proceeded one step further and theorized that if they could learn something as complicated as a language, perhaps they could learn to play the violin. Upon returning home to Japan, he began teaching preschoolers to play the violin. He found to his chagrin that they didn't learn as quickly as he had hoped. Why, he wondered, could children learn a language from their mothers with relative ease, yet be slower in learning to play the violin when taught by him.

Eventually, it dawned upon him—he was teaching the wrong students. He should first teach the mothers who, in turn, could teach their youngsters. And so began what is now known as the Suzuki mother-tongue method of teaching.

Suzuki's Mother-Tongue Language Method

At first the children were allowed only to watch their mothers during classes and while they practiced. After about three months the children were permitted to try their own hands on the bow and strings. In a very short time the children's abilities surpassed those of their mothers.

At that time, most music teachers insisted that a student needed at least three years of lessons before he could be expected to produce good tones. In 1942, the audiences at the Hibiya Auditorium in Tokyo were astonished to hear thirty Suzuki-trained children, ages four to nine, play a Seitz concert after having had only one year of lessons.

I should like to stress that these tiny musicians were not playing a simplified version of "Twinkle, Twinkle Little Star." I attended a concert of Suzuki children at Carnegie Hall in 1973. These youngsters played Brahms, Mozart, Chopin, and so on. Only the heights of the musicians and the lengths of their violins were small. The sounds they made were rich and full. The finale was grand indeed. Twelve American children joined the Japanese children on stage and began playing their violins. Then another twelve stepped on stage. And then another dozen. Finally at least two hundred and fifty children filled the stage.

The Suzuki method is known and used throughout the world. It is estimated that there over eight thousand youngsters in the United States studying under Suzuki's mother-tongue method.

"Teaching music is not our main purpose," Suzuki says. "I want to make good citizens. If a child hears good music from the day of his birth, and learns to play it himself, he develops sensitivity, discipline, and endurance. He gets a beautiful heart."

The Rapidly Diminishing Advice and Dissent

It is difficult to believe, in the light of recent evidence which indicates that children learn a great deal in their early years, that there are still those people who cling to past illusions. Perhaps they have gripped the shattered ropes of outmoded philosophies for so long that it is impossible for them to let go and open either their hands or their minds to new approaches.

Within the last year, a book entitled *Don't Push Your Pre-schooler* was published. In the book, the author infers that a great deal of harm can be done to the child if his parents *force* him to spend hours and hours in academic pursuits. I agree wholeheartedly with that. I'm sure Glenn Doman does too. And Bloom. And most of the others who champion early learning. All would agree that children should not be taught *anything* by the pressure-cooker method. However, the idea that young children require hours and hours of drill in order to learn is as erroneous as the flat world theory. Before the age of six, children learn so quickly and easily that hours and hours of regimental tedium are not necessary; they are, in fact, detrimental.

What is most annoying about such books is the professional put-down of parents' abilities and common sense. The attitude is that parents should leave their children alone until the "educator"—that professional with a degree—can teach them properly. So little respect is shown to the innate abilities and judgment of parents.

The proposition that parents' highest capabilities are composed of playing patty-cake with their babies and teaching them to tie their shoelaces is nauseating. Most of the parents I know are very bright and quite perceptive; and by the way, they love their children, which is certainly more than I can say for many of the teachers I meet.

What a tremendous advantage it would be if we could somehow erase all the nonsense from our minds concerning the abilities of children and the capabilities of parents which for so long has blurred our vision, numbed our intuition, and polluted our thinking. Of course this isn't completely possible. Merlin is no longer with us. So, we must squarely face these myths, one by one, and sort the fact from the fiction, the wit from the whim, and the sense from the nonsense.

If the sole purpose of this writing was to tell you how you could teach your preschooler, it would be a worthwhile undertaking. But the *whys* are as important as the *hows*. In all probability, the *whys* are even more important. If we explored only the *hows,* then you would be limited to following step by step procedures, but if we embrace the *whys* then you will more fully realize the unlimited potentials your child possesses, and will eagerly utilize your own thoughts and innovations in teaching your child.

Goals are terribly important. Your goal should be more than merely teaching your child basic rules of order. Your goal is to help him become a self-sufficient human being. Often goals conceived by parents for their children are much clearer than those set by educators. The kindergarten teacher will tell you that her goal is to prepare the child for the first grade. The first grade teacher will state that her goal is to prepare the student for the second grade, the second grade is to prepare him for the third grade, and on and on and on. Such standard-setters are myopic in their vision.

Parents are not so nearsighted. Parents realize that the intervening years between birth and adulthood encompass the preparation of a person. And they are right. They believe that their child has the innate potential to become whatever he chooses. They encourage their children to dream their dreams and to set the loftiest of goals.

Sad to say, it is sometimes the teacher, in later years, who begins to limit the child. An English teacher recently told me that his goal was to teach children proper sentence structure and word usage, not to turn them into professional writers. Such a man has no business standing in front of a class of children. He should be placed in the back room of a warehouse, sorting eggs and labeling crates.

Today there should be no doubt that, before the age of six, children have the amazing ability to absorb astounding quantities of information. We should not be required to prove this over and over and over. It is a truth.

However, it is fair to ask:

•Is early learning *good* for children?
•If it is good for them, who should teach them?
•What should they be taught?
•How soon should we start teaching them?
•What are the best methods for teaching preschoolers?

These are proper questions that deserve answers. We don't have to wait for the twenty-first century to find them. They are already available to us. The answers are ours for the taking.

Chapter 3

Unraveling the Riddles
of Childhood Development

Millions of Years —
Billions of Brain Cells

Intelligence is no human sideshow but an evolutionary
main event.

—ROBERT ARDREY
African Genesis[1]

Now is the time to buckle our seat belts and hang on to our
armchairs!

Within the following pages, we are going to explore some
of the most significant information pertaining to why very
young children can learn at amazingly rapid rates. It is going
to be a trip from the unknown into the known; a journey
through millions of years into billions of brain cells. It will
be a safari through the jungles of Man's past and a rare
glimpse into Mankind's future.

In the course of these pages we will examine the anthropo-
logical stages of Man: his evolutionary past, his biological
structure, and his neurological development. Most important, we will discover what children really are, how they
develop, how they learn, and what great potentials they possess. We will also explore how we can increase the learning
capacities of young children and improve their abilities.

It may be a bumpy trip; one that will jar your thinking and

accelerate your circulation, ignite your curiosity, whet your intellectual appetite, and widen the horizons of the goals you set for you and your child. In short, you may never again be the same. And you may never again look upon children in the same way you have in the past.

Clear the Track of Ancient Debris

If we intend to look at children properly, there are two obstacles we must hurdle:

Obstacle Number One: The view that the child is a product of two parents and indirectly the product of four grandparents.

That is certainly a narrow view of the child's lineage, allowing us only a limited view of him through tunnel vision, obscuring our appraisal of the vastness of potentials which are inherently his. Actually, our children are not mere products of a mother and a father, but are the result of Mankind, and millions of years of evolutionary development and sociological structures.

Obstacle Number Two: The view that the child's physical abilities are easily observable but that his brain function is not.

We have been led to believe, or have deluded ourselves into believing, that brain function is an intangible, remote and hidden from the eyes and ears of the average person. We tend to think that only psychologists or those persons with a Ph.D. attached to their names could possibly understand or observe the brain function of human beings. This is, of course, absurd. Brain function is not a remote intangible hidden in the confines of our heads. We can readily see it and hear it and feel it, not only in ourselves, but we can watch it work in others. For instance, when we see a child run across the yard we may say, "Johnny's arms and legs are getting stronger everyday," or "Janey's body is becoming more agile." Both statements may be true, but they are extremely limited views of what is being witnessed.

We don't really believe that Johnny's arms and legs control his running, now do we? And we don't really believe that Janey's agility is simply a result of muscle tone and growth, do we? Of course not. Johnny's arms and legs are not moving just because they have grown bigger and stronger; they are moving because he has a brain. And Janey is not more agile because her body is better coordinated. She is more agile because her brain is in better control of her body. What we are really witnessing are the demonstrations of Johnny's and Janey's brain functions.

In fact, when we watch a child doing whatever he is doing —stacking blocks, looking at books, turning somersaults— we are observing not only his eyes and hands and arms and legs in motion, we are watching the results of his brain functions.

In order to alter our views, it is terribly important that we remove these obstacles.

A Journey into the Known Unknown

People's reactions to ideas and philosophies constantly amaze me. About two years ago, I was sitting in a rather posh French café in New York with a senior editor for a large publishing firm. We were discussing the possibility of his publishing a series of books on childhood development. Glenn Doman was to write the books and I was to illustrate them.

About halfway through a fillet of sole, the editor said, "Oh, by the way, there should be no mention of evolution in these books."

I couldn't believe my ears.

"Even the mention of such radical theories," he explained between bites, "will turn off a large audience of people— especially in the Bible Belt."

I asked how he proposed that we compare the biological

development of the individual to the development of the species without the mention of evolution.

He quickly agreed that we could not, then, just as quickly, asserted that we should not make reference to Charles Darwin, nor to Raymond Dart. Of course, for the same reasons —the Bible Belt.

I had been led to believe that the Scopes trial was past history, but I wondered if it were about to be reopened.

"You understand," he said, apologetically, "I believe in evolution" (as if it were a newfound religion), "but I wouldn't want our sales potential to be lessened in any way because it was mentioned."

Sitting before me was a well-educated world traveler—a highly literate man who was in the business of publishing information—telling me that ideas were too hot to handle and that book sales meant more to him than did either logic or reason. I was stunned. And I still am when I think about his comments.

Before we go any further—I am not an atheist—thank God. I believe in God as surely as I believe in light and sound. So if you are of the Bible Belt, tighten your buckle, and hang in here a little longer.

The conversation with the publisher disturbed me because here was a sophisticated New Yorker explaining the attitudes of the Bible Belt to me—a boy from Springfield, Missouri, reared as a Southern Baptist, which is about as fundamental a group as one can find. I grew up on "hellfire and brimstone" Sunday morning sermons. By the time I was ten years of age, I could probably quote more verses from the Scriptures than many adults have ever read.

I have never understood why there has been such an uproar and such animosity over the theory of evolution because I have never been able to see that the evolutionary creation was any less spectacular or less of a miracle than was the seven-day version. In fact, I have felt that the scientific discoveries of the universe broadened Man's concept of God rather than diminished it in any way. I have believed that the

Bible was a collection of inspired writings which were translated into terms that Man could understand at the time that they were written.

In speaking of evolution, it is not my intention to begin a religious argument. The same would apply if I wrote of Genesis; I would not be trying to initiate a scientific argument. One has only to read the newspapers to realize that the world is still in the process of creation—volcanoes erupt forming new land masses, earthquakes and floods inundate other areas. I think it is obvious that the creation did not end on the seventh day, but it has been a continuing process.

There is so much evidence that species develop through evolutionary phases in order to adapt to the environment. We would have to hide our heads in the sand and close our ears to any longer discount such probabilities. As God was —God is. As creation was—creation is. As evolution was— evolution is.

In light of recent scientific and empirical evidence, to present the physical and intellectual development of children without regarding the evolutionary development of the species of Man would be neither scientific nor even reasonable. If we do not use the brains we were given or have developed, then what purpose do they serve?

My editor friend in New York was more interested in mass sales than he was in accuracy. During lunch, he had proved himself unworthy to publish information about children. The thought that any information need be watered down for the sake of popularity nauseates me. If the mention of evolution is the most unpopular statement in this writing, then I am either extremely lucky or I have not expressed other opinions clearly enough.

However, because the information I am about to present concerning how children learn and why the younger they are the faster they learn is so important, I hope that the reader will not turn away without considering these things.

Now, let's get on with it.

The Age of Dart

Dr. Raymond A. Dart, a legend in his own lifetime, has long been recognized as one of the great anthropologists of all time. Dr. Dart is the discoverer of *Australopithecus,* whose fossil bones prove that Man's ancestors walked upright on earth more than a million years ago. In his book *Adventures with the Missing Link,* Dr. Dart writes:

> The greatest questions man has ever posed or is ever likely to pose are these that we have been attempting to answer: Whence has man come? How was he made? How did he come to differ from other creatures? How is it that he at first learned so little and then came, as it were in a series of sudden spurts, to know so much about the world and himself while other living creatures were content simply to live and to remain ignorant?[2]

In the realm of medical research, Dr. Temple Fay, the famed neurosurgeon, realized the great need for probing into Man's evolutionary past. In the book *Temple Fay, M.D.,* compiled by James M. Wolf, Ed.D., Dr. Fay writes:

> In the study of the origin and evolution of human patterns of movement, one is immediately faced with a fantastically extended time scale. The process of natural selection, adaption and discard of unfavorable species, structural misfits, or neurological responses not desirable or retainable, had ample time to accomplish the present human model of movement and locomotion.[3]

"All living organisms go through a developmental process of organization which in vertebrates, as in other phyla, begins with the union of the ovum and the sperm," writes Dr. Edward B. LeWinn, M.D., in his book *Human Neurological Organization.* During this developmental process, "there emerge in each system, and thus in the whole organism, the forms and characteristics of the species. Along the way, to some degree, recognizable traces of earlier and more primitive structures and functions of the evolutionary forebears of the species are detectable. Thus, in its development the human organism fleetingly displays representations of some of the characteristics of its predecessors in the vertebrate phylum; for example, the gill of the fish, the patterns of movement of the reptile."[4]

It is an established fact that at one stage in development the human fetus has gills, and it is obvious that its intrauterine environment is aquatic. After birth, the infant continues through the evolutionary stages of mobility development—crawling, reflective of the salamander stage; creeping, the quadruped; and walking, the primate. We see the history of evolution repeat itself in each child's development. Millions of years crystalize into months.

"The human baby, the human being, is a mosaic of animal and angel," observes J. Bronowski in his book *The Ascent of Man*. "Every human action goes back in some part to our animal origins; we should be cold and lonely creatures if we were cut off from that bloodstream of life."[5]

It is extremely important for us to consider that children are the result of the schema of Mankind rather than the mere offspring of two adults, because of excluding his entire heritage, too often, far too often, we limit his potentialities by considering only those of his progenitors. For instance, if the father is athletic, then we're not at all surprised that the son likes to play baseball. If the mother is an actress, then we are inclined to suspect that some inborn talents have been genetically passed on to the child.

The same is true in regard to deficiencies. If the father is an illiterate day-laborer and the child has problems in learning to read, we tend to say, "What can you expect?" If the mother is neurotic and the daughter doesn't relate well to the society around her, then we smirk and say, "Like mother, like daughter."

This is a terrible way to look at children. It is both demeaning and damaging.

If we took newborn babies and switched their environments—let us say, we gave a New York City child to a set of primitive parents in New Guinea; and a primitive baby to a set of Russian peasants; and we gave the Russian peasant baby to a set of London intellectuals, and gave the London intellectual baby to a set of itinerent farm laborers; and we gave the itinerent farm laborers' baby to the New York City parents, and then asked, "Will these children grow up to be like their parents?" one would be led to ask, "Which parents? The real parents or the adopted parents?"

If we say, "The real parents," he would answer, "Of course not."

If we say, "The adopted parents," he would reply, "Yes, the children will probably grow up to be like them."

If he holds any reservations in his mind it will probably be that he might believe that the baby from the more sophisticated culture might do better in the less sophisticated culture than would the child from the more primitive culture who is transplanted into the more "academically inclined" family. Intellectually, we could convince ourselves that this isn't true, but because we can't sweep all the cobwebs of past misconceptions out of our heads, emotionally, we are influenced by such poppycock. The truth is, and many, many studies attest to this fact, children adapt to the culture in which they are reared whether that culture be primitive or sophisticated, or anywhere in between.

If the genes passed on to children are the limiting factors of their abilities or disabilities, then how could this be true? It could not be. A child's genetic heritage is the result of millions of years and trillions of right choices. He is a product of Mankind. If he is born with set potentialities, those inborn potentialities are not limited to those his immediate parents possess. He is born with the potentialities that all children possess. It is the sociological and environmental limitations to which children are forced to adapt.

So let's discard from our minds that New York City children have inborn New York City potentialities, or that New Guinea children have inborn New Guinea potentialities, or that our neighbors' children have inborn neighbors' potentialities. Or that your children have the inborn potentialities of their father and mother. Children have the inborn potentialities of human beings—not just those of their parents; they are related to all people. Within their lineage are the Einsteins, the Churchills, the Shakespeares, the Shaws, the Steinbecks, the Kellers, the Aristotles, the Michaelangelos. Children have in their family heritage the greatest geniuses the world has ever known.

The Sensuous Saga of the Human Brain

"With respect to human beings," says Scott Crossfield, X-15 pilot, "where else would you get a nonlinear computer weighing only 160 pounds, having a billion binary decision elements that can be mass produced by unskilled labor?"[6]

In the mechanical sense, a baby is a marvelous piece of machinery with a multitude of moving parts which can be moved individually or in concert. A baby is able to take in food and dispense vital energy through an intricate system of arteries and veins to the needed organs. Not only is its whole exterior covered with an elaborate system of nerve endings for sensing the slightest touch, but the baby is also equipped with a sound receiving system and an audio output mechanism that astound the imagination. When these components are properly formed, wired, and geared, the child is superior to all machines, will surpass all other animals—for he will be able to adjust to any surroundings. He not only hears meaningful sounds but is able to discern meanings, nuances, and emotions. His complex responses are able to communicate emotion in its widest range from anger to love, from pain to physical pleasure—and, ultimately, to fulfill the hope of Man, that he will be able to express himself to others.

For inside this tiny head is the marvel of marvels—that

spongy mass of cells that will store knowledge, discern and discriminate, calculate and assimilate information, and command all working parts of his being—the brain.

It amazes me that in vast volumes of books which are published on the subjects of education, academic achievement, and learning so few of them even mention the brain. They so often read as if hearing is a function of the ears, that reading is a function of the eyes, that talking is a function of the mouth, that writing is a function of the hands, that coordination is a function of the body, and that feeling is a function of the skin. It is as if these authors are asserting that a child's ears have to learn to understand words, that a child's mouth has to learn how to speak, that a child's hand has to learn how to write, that a child's body has to learn to turn somersaults, and that a child's skin has to learn how to touch. Isn't it obvious that hands, mouths, eyes, ears, noses, and thoughts do not learn anything? It is the brain that learns. It is the brain that thinks. It is the brain that must be taught. Without a functioning brain, a hand is no more than a piece of meat, eyes and ears are useless receptors, the mouth is a silent voice box. Without the brain there is no learning. Without the brain there is no child.

How is it possible to discuss learning without regard for that organ of learning—the brain? It is not. To do so would be like discussing the circulatory system without mentioning the heart. It would be like discussing the ocean without mentioning water. It would be like discussing our solar system without mentioning the sun.

"The shiny, wrinkled jelly of the human brain . . . is more intricate and effective than any other work of nature," writes Adrian Hope. "Whether we are awake or asleep, its electro-chemical network of ten billion nerve cells maintains a ceaseless activity, running the myriad functions of the body (breathing alone requires the complex coordination of 90 muscles) and analyzing raw sense data from the outside world. . . . The brain can process hundreds of bits of information at a time, and it can sedulously distinguish between reality and memory and fantasy. It has even developed the capacity to control—at least in part—the very drives and emotions that it spawns."[7]

The human brain is protected by a life support system that favors it over every other organ in the body. Encased in bone to shield its soft tissue, the brain is bathed in cerebrospinal fluid to protect it against impact. Although it makes up only 2 percent of the body's total weight, it receives 20 percent of the body's oxygen. The brain also receives a highly disproportionate share of nutriments. Even in cases of malnutrition, it has been found that although a child may weigh half the normal weight, his brain may be only 15 percent below the norm.

"There are approximately one hundred billion cells in every child's head," says Glenn Doman. "At least ten billion of these are neurons of nerve cells capable of functioning as operating units of the brain. Ten billion is a difficult number to associate with reality even for an American taxpayer. To try to give some reality to this number it is helpful to know that if your child had been born before Christ and used a brand-new brain cell every ten seconds, sixty seconds a minute, sixty minutes an hour, twenty-four hours a day, three hundred and sixty-five days a year, and if that child were still alive today, he would have more than three billion neurons which he hadn't yet used.

"The brain, that most important organ, distinguishes Man from other animals. At conception, a child grows from a microscopic one-cell at a fantastic rate of speed. At the moment of conception, there is actually an explosion into growth—in twelve days, the fetus has a brain and spinal column; in twenty-four days, it has a heart and it's beating; in nine months, it has a weight of seven pounds. However, every day, the rate of growth is less than the day before. Between the ages of seven and eight, a child will grow in size almost the same amount that he will between the ages eight and eighty.

"In the first six years of a child's life, a child learns more, fact for fact, than he will learn in the rest of his life," Doman points out.

"The brain," continues Doman, "is a superb computer. It has a large advantage over its mechanical copies; the more that's put in the human brain, the more it will hold; the more it is used, the better it works. As a computer, the brain must be programmed and information must be fed into it. Everything goes into permanent storage in the brain of a three-year-old; he is being programmed.

"Due to the function of the human brain, Man is set apart from other animals. Only Man stands up and walks in a crosspattern. Only Man talks in abstract symbolic language (the good Lord gave Man a superb brain for practical language; Man invented languages like French, German, English). Only Man sees in such a way he can read that language. Only Man hears in such a way he can understand that language when it is spoken. Only Man can oppose his thumb to his forefinger and, using these skills, can write that language. Only Man can feel an object and know what it is without smelling, seeing, or tasting it.

"In other words, there are six functions that characterize Man—walking, talking, writing, reading, hearing, and feeling."[8]

Although modern science has probed the complexities of the human brain, charting its structure, chemistry, and functions, still no one knows exactly how the brain learns. Doman believes that the nervous system of each human being must develop through a series of stages before the brain can function to its fullest potential. In effect, these stages of development repeat in telescoped time the evolution of Man: from lower forms to the unique human achievements of abstract thought and speech, reading, writing, and language. Ontogeny repeats phylogeny—the life history of the individual repeats that of the species.

Many scoffed at Dr. Temple Fay's theories of the evolutionary stages of the brain, but now, after his death, others are drawing the same conclusions.

In his article "The Uncommitted Cortex," Wilder Penfield, M.D., writes: "What the brain is allowed to record, how and when it is conditioned—these things prepare it for great achievement, or limit it to mediocrity. Boy and man are capable of so much more than is demanded of them! Adjust the time and the manner of learning; then you may double your demands and your expectations."[9]

"The function of the brain is to relate its owner to his environment," Doman stresses. "The degree of efficiency with which that brain relates its owner to his environment is that child's degree of *neurological organization.*"

A couple of years ago, a friend and I were comparing brain function to a computer. My daughter, who was thirteen at the time, listened for a while and then said, "I don't think my brain functions like a computer."

"Of course it does," I insisted. "For instance, visualize in your mind what your room looks like. Do you see it?"

"It's pretty messy," she grinned.

"But do you see it?"

"I see it."

"What things are on your desk?"

She listed about thirty items, from pencils to hairpins.

"Now visualize your closet and tell us everything you can remember that is inside."

The list grew even longer and rivaled the contents of Fibber McGee's closet in both quantity and clutter (the sack of bird seed which was supposed to be in the storeroom was located, and the brown belt I had been searching for was found).

"Now tell me what books you have in your bookcase."

She recalled the titles and authors of approximately fifty books which ranged in taste from classic to trash.

"Could you give us a synopsis of each one of those books?"

"If you'd care to listen for about three hours, I probably could," she replied.

"Don't you see how many thousands of pieces of information you have inside of your head? We could go on and on.

I could ask you about items in the kitchen cabinets, and the living room, the yard, the neighborhood, your school, and I could ask you questions about movies and television. You could pour out millions and millions of pieces of information because your brain has received and categorized all of those things like a computer."

I waited for an exclamation from her or at least the expression of a new awareness.

"If I have such a neat brain, and I can keep all of those things in order, why is my room so messy?" she wanted to know.

"Because you didn't do what your mother told you to this morning."

"Right on, Dad."

We really take brain function for granted. If we sat down and started making a list of all the pieces of information stored in our heads, we would never be able to complete it. Our fingers would wear out before we really got started. The same is true of a preschooler—his list is growing so fast everyday that by three years of age, his knowledge of the world around him far exceeds the things you could write down in ten years. Amazing indeed!

In the book *Children of Dreams—Children of Hope,* Raymundo Veras, M.D., offers a description of brain function in prose that touches poetry:

> The brain is like the earth. The earth is big but the brain is bigger. The earth is one of many planets within the universe but the brain is cosmic. As far as Man can reach out into the universe so can he reach just as far into the brain. The brain is not only information—it is imagination. It is both precise and precious. It is both a storage place and a source of information. It is both fact and fiction. Yesterday and today—the past and the future.[10]

Growing a Child's Brain

Glenn Doman once told me that there is a secret in his book *How to Teach Your Baby to Read* that many mothers discover. In some of the thousands of letters he receives, mothers write: "I taught my three-year-old to read, and I noticed that when he learned to read his physical coordination improved" or "when my child learned to read, I think her hearing improved" or "when my child learned to read, his speech improved." Repeatedly, they asked, "Do you think that there is any connection between the two?"

When Glenn showed me some of these letters he said, "Look at how bright these women are. Aren't they great? They caught on. Of course the answer is 'yes' in every case. But these women already knew it."

Doman continued, "Everything we do to alter the function of the brain has the potential to alter the other functions. But that's just part of the secret. The rest of the secret is that there is a good deal of research which indicates that we are not only improving the function of the brain, but we are actually *growing* the brain.

"Can you imagine the excitement that all mothers could have when teaching their young children if they knew that not only were they turning their kid on to information but at the same time, they were actually growing their child's brain?"

Doman is not saying that mothers are growing only that intangible thing called "mind." Nor is he saying that they are growing only that intangible thing called "capacity for learning." Beyond growing both the mind and the learning capacity, scientific evidence indicates that they are also growing that physical thing called the brain.

As David Krech writes concerning his research with rats:

This we do know: permitting the young IC (Isolated Control) rat to grow up in a psychologically impoverished environment creates an animal with a relatively deteriorated brain—a brain with a relatively thin and light cortex, lowered blood supply, diminished enzymatic activities, smaller neuronal cell bodies, and fewer glia cells. A lack of adequate psychological fare for the young animal results in palpable, measurable, deteriorative changes in the brain's chemistry and anatomy.

Although we have worked only with rats, it is not unfair to ask whether our findings might also be applied to the human condition. Certainly we know that, among people, early cultural environments can range from the highly challenging to the severely impoverished. Although it would be scientifically unjustified to conclude at this stage that our results do apply to people, it would, I think, be socially criminal to assume that they do *not* apply—and, so assuming, fail to take account of the implications.[11]

When Dr. Krech was in Philadelphia in 1969 to receive the Human Potential Award from The Institutes in recognition for his work in advancing the knowledge of Mankind, Glenn Doman asked him what conclusions he might have drawn from his work since that writing. Dr. Krech told him that he had established experiments in which rats received early stimulation in cages on moving platforms. When the researchers sacrificed these rats, not only was the quality of their brains better, but they were measurably larger and weighed more than did those of the rats that were not stimulated. However, Krech said that they took these experiments one step further. Realizing that a rat's ultimate function was that of a searcher, his staff built mazes and placed a third group of rats in those where they were allowed to search for food. The maze box did not move—only the rats moved through the corridors, finding their way—search ng. When these rats were sacrificed, the researchers found that the brains of these rats were even larger and heavier, and were of better quality than those that were stimulated on the moving platforms. Dr. Krech said these findings indicated to the researchers that when members of a species were allowed or encouraged to perform their ultimate function that the size, the quality, and the weight of their brains could be increased.

Now what does this have to do with people? According to Dr. Krech, if we look at Man and how these findings would apply to him, we should first consider what is Man's ultimate function. What one thing is Man capable of performing which is unique and his alone? Krech said the answer is obvious—language. Only Man has a language—a reading, hearing, speaking, writing language. He said it appeared to him that during early stages of development, if children have the opportunity and are encouraged to perform their ultimate function, utilizing that reading, hearing, speaking, writing language, their brains grow larger, become heavier, and even the structural qualities are improved.

Now, if you have a child under six years of age, doesn't this information make you want to call him to you or make you want to run to where he is and take a look at his head? And when you look at his head, won't you be looking at it differently than you ever have before? First of all you'll be looking at the confines of a potential genius. For now you know that it is possible for you to help his brain grow by giving him more information.

The search to learn more about brain-injured children, and indeed, all children, has led Glenn Doman, Carl Delacato, and the staff members of The Institutes to circle the earth twice within the last three years. They have lived with and studied Xinguana children in Brazil Centrale, the Bushmen in the Kalahari Desert, the Eskimos in the Arctic, and the Navajos in Arizona, as well as children in countless other urban, suburban, rural, and primitive communities throughout the world.

"It is evident to us," Doman says, "if we are concerned with childhood development, that we must know as much as possible about all children—not just Philadelphia children, not just American children—but all children.

"Without knowing it," continues Doman, "the brain-injured children and their parents have performed a great service for all the children of the world. Through them we have learned successful ways to increase the abilities of not only brain-injured children but, indeed, all children. If these methods to accelerate childhood development and brain growth are made available to well children, their potential for learning staggers the imagination."

For Doman and his staff to be able to work with these children and to train their parents to accelerate their growth patterns both physically and academically at faster rates than well children develop is phenomenal.

"Yet how many times," says Doman, "do you think you could watch a brain-injured child grow faster than a well child, or how many times could you see a three-year-old brain-injured child reading before you asked yourself, 'what's wrong with the well kids?'

"Well, the answer is obvious, or at least, it was to us—the brain-injured kids were reading because they were given the opportunity to read and they were growing at astounding rates because we had given them an environment which was inducive to the acceleration of their opportunities to achieve. The truth is that when you give a brain-injured kid a stimulating environment he often gets better and when you put a well kid in a lousy environment he doesn't do very well. If you place a well kid in a mediocre environment his achievement most often is mediocre, but if you place a well kid in a stimulating environment conducive to learning, then watch him go—those kids are called genius!"

What's wrong with the average child? Not much. He really does fairly well when considering that we often keep information from him during the years in which it is easiest for him to learn. In truth, we have frequently done all we can do to retard the learning of an "average" child. Small wonder he's called "average." What a pity! He might have been so much more.

Superb Pieces of Humanity

If we have done so poorly with the average child's neurological development and education in this country and throughout the world, what can we do about it?

The first step in rectifying past errors is to recognize that we *have* done so poorly.

Some time in the past we must have assumed that, like the common man, God must have loved average children because he made so many of them. Actually God gives us superb pieces of humanity—it is adults who reduce them to average human beings.

If we want to justify our past errors by saying we did not know any better, then well and good. For in truth, we did not know better. But in the light of present research and scientific information, what excuse can we now offer if we choose to ignore it?

In the past we have taken an extremely dim view of children. For the most part we loved them and wanted them to be happy, but we also concluded that they were the way they were because that's the way they were and that's the way the world has always been. We were told by the professionals that children grew and matured in certain God-planned time frames and that there was little we could do to improve their lot. We were often told that tender loving care and a lot of patience would help them to be content with their inadequacies as they grew taller. We believed what we were told and the professionals believed those things they were telling us.

The educators told us that we could do irreparable harm if we tried to teach the child rather than just train him. They inferred that each child was born with limitations on his capacity to learn and that his "intelligence quotient" was set at birth by certain genetic endowments, and that his learning potential could not be altered no matter what we did. To expect more from a child than mispronounced words and jumbled sentences might tend to frustrate him and mar his self-image for life.

Surely from what we have seen, we are now aware of the great sadness in those pieces of advice. We have become aware that the brain is like a computer; that it will receive billions of pieces of information and the more information it receives, the wider is its capacity to receive still more. We have seen that by five years of age, fact for fact, a child has 80 percent of the knowledge that he will acquire during his entire life. We have seen that babies have the ability to be linguistic geniuses; they can learn three languages—six languages—with the same ease with which they can learn one. It has been proposed that geniuses are not made in the womb, but that they are a result of having had the opportunity to learn at very young ages.

If all these things are true, and indications certainly appear that they are, doesn't it turn your stomach to realize that we have been told to keep our children dumb and innocent of information until they enter school?

As you look at your child's head aren't you led to wonder how well you have ignited his learning capacity and how well you have grown those neurons encased within his skull? Doesn't the thought make you break out in a cold sweat and isn't there a knot gnawing in the pit of your stomach? But when you think of all the potentialities that you now have to nurture your child's growth, doesn't it fill your body with new excitement? It certainly should!

The Pressures of Time—The Dictates of Conscience

In the last eight years it has been my extreme pleasure and anxiety to have been allowed to witness much of this information as it was being put into order. It has been as frustrating an experience as it has been invigorating.

Realizing that he had assembled vast amounts of information that were applicable not only to brain-injured children but to all children, Glenn Doman knew there was an urgent need to make this information available to mothers.

In 1969, we began designing a series of books on childhood development. Glenn had to maneuver his already impossible schedule to allow for days or evenings when he could write. I would fly to Philadelphia to review information and to present the visual layouts to him. If we could manage three consecutive work days together we felt they were a luxury. The project progressed as long as we could steal time. Then it would stop for months when there was no time left to take.

I have little patience for people who mention, as they sip a martini, that they would write a book if they only had the time. They have no idea of what time is. It also occurs to me that it is not the people who have time who write books; it most often is those people who do not. There are limits to energy, but again and again I watched as Glenn pushed himself beyond those limits. It was fascinating to work with him. I've never seen a mind that can absorb information so quickly and can organize it so clearly; he can reduce the most complicated concepts to the simplest of terms.

In one of these sessions, he asked me to draw a typical one-year-old, standing up with his arms in a balance position —a typical toddler. When I finished, he instructed me to draw an eight-year-old child in proportion to the one-year-old. In other words, taller, longer arms, and longer legs, but he told me that he wanted this child standing in the same position as the one-year-old.

When it was completed, he said, "Now, take a good look at those two children. First look at the one-year-old. Cute, isn't he? Taking his first steps, weaving back and forth from side to side, but that's all right because his mother knows that soon he will be walking better. To watch that kid is a real joy for her. That's a kid any mother would be happy to have.

"But now look at the eight-year-old. He's exactly like the one-year-old only he's bigger—he's an eight-year-old toddler —he's brain-injured. What is charming in the stance of the one-year-old is awkward in the eight-year-old. There's not any mother in the world who wouldn't be reduced to tears if she saw her child in that state.

"The real problem for that eight-year-old is that the medical world sees him as an awkward, stumbling eight-year-old and decides that that's the way he is and that's the way he will always be. But they see the one-year-old and say, 'that's a great kid!' That's a tragic injustice because that eight-year-old is just as great as that one-year-old, but his time frames of development haven't been the same. Don't you see that?

"If both of these kids are going to be normal ten-year-olds, and that certainly should be the goal, then the eight-year-old has only two years to make it. But he has to pick up seven years of development in those two years. The reason the one-year-old looks so cute is that we know he has nine years and we see no reason why he won't continue to develop, year by year.

"Now, if we can accelerate that brain-injured eight-year-old's development to increase nine years in a two-year period, and as you know, we do this at The Institutes all the time, doesn't it make you wonder why it takes that healthy one-year-old nine years to accomplish the same thing? In fact, the one-year-old should be able to accomplish stages of development easier and quicker because he has everything going for him.

"We can move that eight-year-old up the stages of development because we structure his environment with intensity, frequency and duration of stimuli. But the environments of most one-year-olds are low-key and not very stimulating. He has to pick up information as he can because adults have this insane idea that they have to keep secrets from him. Only when it's convenient for them will they stimulate his brain. And as you well know, it's not often convenient for them because they have plans of their own. They keep him in a cage called a playpen—playpen, indeed—it's a prison of structured deprivation, and they surround him with the dullest pieces of nonsense. They repeat the dumbest things to him. That kid has to *work* to learn. He has to literally pry information out of them. It's a great sadness and a monumental form of insanity."

He sat down and reflected. "It's not the mothers' fault—they don't know any better. They don't mean to keep their children ignorant. They have been told to give their kids the cutesy toys and to bore them silly with repetition. It's a great sadness—a sadness, indeed."

Those who have had the opportunity to work with a man of conscience must know that it can also be a frustrating experience. You can argue finances with a man who works for monetary gain. You can flatter a man who thrives on attention and strives for public acclaim. But there is no way to sway a man of conscience from a course he feels he must travel.

After months of work and torturous schedules, Doman suddenly called a halt to the project. As he told me his reasons, he paced the floor and, periodically, his hand rubbed his forehead. "As important as this information is," he said, "I simply can't go on with it at this time. I have allowed myself to forget or to at least sidetrack my first obligation—and that, of course, is to the brain-injured children. There is not one shred of information, nor one idea, that I have that has not come through them. As fascinated as I am in seeing mothers of well children accelerate their children's development, I simply can't allow myself the luxury of that fascination—not if I'm going to live with myself. I have to place priorities where they belong. My first priority must be to complete a definitive book on brain injury. I have no other choice. These other books will have to wait."

I sat there and looked about the room. There was not one wall that was not crowded with visual materials, not one table without stacks of manuscripts and illustrations—even the floor had its share of accumulated piles of information. Those volumes of papers and charts represented months and months of work and years and years of this man's search. But now they had to wait. He was right, of course, but that didn't stay the tears in our eyes or the weight that lodged in our chests.

Now, five years later, his book, *What to Do About Your Brain-Injured Child,* is completed. I know the stolen hours and the sleepless nights that went into its creation. I also know the threats those hours posed to his health. But it is done. And soon, I hope that the materials we developed will again be lined around the walls, stacked on the table tops, and heaped on the floor, and we will be at it again.

Those five years have also taken their toll on me. I've moved from project to project, from book to book, but everytime I saw a group of children coming out of school or a toddler at the supermarket, or everytime I saw a baby sucking a pacifier, I churned inside.

I found myself telling friends and acquaintances who had small children, "Say, if you would teach him to read you would grow his brain." They often smiled, cajolingly, and replied, "Oh, of course it will." And then they would glance across the room at someone else and their eyes would agree that I was ready for the funny farm.

Or I'd walk into a friend's home and see a toddler sitting in a playpen and I'd say, "You know, it's none of my business, but he'd learn a helluva lot more if you'd let him out of that thing." And they would agree that it was, indeed, none of my business and explain that if they let him out he would roam throughout the house, picking up things and looking at them. When I would answer that that is called experience and learning, they often retorted that it was also called "breaking" and "nuisance."

There were times when I had this great urge to carry a sledge hammer with me, and whenever I saw a playpen I dreamed that I would smash it with one swift blow, and yell, "Save the children!" But I didn't. Instead, I'd just say, "Sorry, kid. I tried."

But how many times can one say, "Sorry, kid, I tried" without either going berserk or insane? Not many.

Sometimes I would be talking with teachers and I would

say, "Listen, do you know that five-year-olds can learn faster than six-year-olds?" And without the least trace or even a glimmer of understanding they would answer, "Isn't that interesting." I felt like screaming, "You're goddamned right that's interesting, and if you want to know something fascinating, four-year-olds can learn faster then five-year-olds! Now doesn't that curdle your yogurt?"

But I didn't. I would just stand there with all of these thoughts pent up inside of me.

Then I began to realize that Glenn Doman had not done me a favor. He had introduced me to all of this information and I had to live with it bottled up within me.

Everytime I picked up a newspaper I would read about the crappy things we are doing to children. I would read reports about the slave systems called schools, and read another doctor's advice to mothers, telling them that they should love their children and get away from them as fast as they can.

If you had read about a man standing on the street corner, yelling, "Save the children!" that would have been me.

And if you had read about a woman standing by my side trying to console me, that would have been my wife.

And if you had read about troops marching in to carry us off, that would have been the army of status quo.

But later, if you had read that groups of toddlers had started breaking their playpens and had begun stealing books, they would have been our revenge.

Compared to Children Adults Are Hopelessly Mentally Retarded

We have just torn down and discarded two archaic myths:

1. Your child's potentialities are not limited by the abilities of his mother and father. Within your child is a genetic endowment from all Mankind. Therefore, he is a potential artist, a potential writer, a potential singer, a potential actor, a potential lawyer, a potential doctor, a potential President

of the United States—or he is a potential day laborer, a potential primitive, or a potential dullard. Worse still, he has the potential to be average. Whatever men and women can achieve, so too does your child have the potential to achieve if he is given the information and the opportunity.

2. Your child's abilities are no mere product of physical growth. They are also a product of brain function. As a computer, the brain can be filled with meaningful information or with useless drivel. If you choose to give him accurate information during the early years of his life, there is a very good possibility that you are not only increasing his awareness, but that in doing so, you are actually growing his brain —that it is increasing in quality, in size, and in weight.

Take a look at your child now. What do you see? I hope you see a cute and cuddly human being who has a superb computer inside his head, eager to be programmed with the best information you can provide. I hope you see more than just a baby who requires washing and feeding and Mother Goose rhymes. I hope you envision that your child has within him the best that Mankind and God have to offer. He has a genius for learning.

In 1970, Glenn Doman had some statements printed on balloons and gave these balloons to children throughout the world. One of the statements read, "Compared to children, adults are hopelessly mentally retarded." When the words were translated to them, the children thought the message was funny. Adults thought it was amusing. But those who knew better knew that it was also true.

Now, dear reader, you have become one of that select group who know—"Compared to children, adults *are* hopelessly mentally retarded."

Chapter 4

How Soon the Three R's?

Maybe We Should Smuggle a Book
Inside the Incubator

Even if we considered them to be nothing more than pets, children are expensive. The emotional price alone taxes the coffers of our patience. Children often require more love than we ever suspected we had to give.

Never before have new parents had anyone or anything that has been so totally dependent upon them:

In the first months of a baby's life, women are turned into nursemaids and bottlewarmers.

The entire household revolves around feeding schedules and diaper changes.

The smell of talcum powder saturates the air.

People who hitherto faced the morning alarm with disdain, jump out of bed almost cheerfully for a two-o'clock feeding.

The torturous hours of colic are endured.

And there are the total joys:

"She turned over by herself, today."

"Today he took his first steps."

"Look at that smile! Now I ask you, has there ever in all the world been a smile like that? No! Never!"

And the pains:

Parents have to witness the tears brought on by burned fingers and bumps to the head.

And they must administer band-aids to scraped knees and elbows.

They endure midnight calls to the doctor for instant advice, and all night vigils with dampened washcloths to soothe a tiny fevered forehead.

Soon there are roller skates outside the door.

And a tricycle.

And before you know it—a bicycle.

Five years of slamming screen doors and peanut butter sandwiches gallop by.

In terms of dollars and cents, children are also extremely costly. The report of the Commission on Population Growth and the American Future published in 1970 states: "Depending on her educational background, a woman's loss of earnings over a period of 14 years due to the birth of her first child might be as high as $58,904 if she is a high school graduate, $82,467 if she has a college degree, and $103,023.00 if she has a post college education. Plus it is estimated that the yearly cost of raising a child (food, clothing, etc.) usurps 15 to 17 percent of the total family income.[1]

Perhaps one of the problems we have in rearing children, is that we don't regard them as financial investments, but tend to view them as commonplace commodities. If we viewed them as financial assets or liabilities, their years and their needs might be tended quite differently and rewarded more respect.

If one child can cost us so much (from $58,904 to $103,023, plus 15 to 17 percent yearly of our family income) during the first fourteen years of his life, we had better pay more than a casual interest to our investment. That's more money than most of us pay for our homes and cars combined. We realize we must keep our houses and automobiles in good condition if resale values are to remain at their peak. If there were an open market for selling kids, perhaps we would use every means to improve our products. Each family would strive to create the healthiest, strongest, brightest kid on the block. If we would do that for money, wouldn't love be a better reason? One would hope so.

Put-downs by Omissions

Apparently, many educators still believe that the parents' prime objective during their children's first five years of life is to prepare their youngsters for the requirements of the classroom. Consequently, in summer issues of women's and parents' magazines and in newspaper columns, lists frequently appear advising parents of those things their child should be able to do by the time school begins. Although words are rearranged to avoid accusations of plagiarism, the contents are usually the same. These are considered to be "The Ten Commandments" for preparing your child for school:

1. Your child should know his name, address, and phone number.
2. He should be able to dress and undress himself.
3. He should know the names of his mother and father and their occupations.
4. He should know how to use the toilet properly and to wash his hands afterward.
5. He must know that he will be expected to ask the teacher's permission before going to the restroom.
6. He must know that he is expected to take his turn, to speak up when asked a question, and understand that he must share toys, materials, and the teacher's attention with the other children.
7. He must know how to get to and from school and to observe necessary safety rules.
8. He should be taught to look upon the teacher as a friend and not be frightened by the teacher's authoritative disciplinary measures.
9. It is wise to let your child meet his teacher and see his classroom before school begins.
10. If possible, accompany your child to school the first day.

Surely, these "ten commandments" were first written by a teacher who thought it over for many days and nights to figure out in her own mind what abilities the children should have when they are placed in her charge. And they are clearly commandments because there are no negotiable clauses and no mention of what the party of the first part (the teacher) will give in return. On faith, parents will hope that she will teach in a friendly and even humane way.

I'm sure that kindergarten and first grade teachers, upon reading such a list, nod their heads in agreement that it is both concise and very good. And I'm just as sure that, come summer, it will reappear in many periodicals.

However, this isn't a good list at all—it's a terrible list! By omissions this list is a great put-down of the abilities of both mothers and children. Most mothers who read it realize that their five-year-olds knew most of these things when they were three, or certainly could have. So what is the list saying?

Is it saying that teachers expect all five-year-olds to be as smart as three-year-olds? Or are they saying that they expect them to be as dumb? Are they concluding that these things are as much as most kids can learn in five years? Or do they believe that these things are all that can be taught by unskilled labor?

The list fails to mention that the child should be able to hear and speak a language. There isn't anything on that list as difficult as learning a language. Certainly learning to wait in line and wash hands isn't nearly as complex as constructing a verbal sentence. Yet mothers are given no credit for having taught their children this extremely complicated skill. On this list, her achievements are reduced to merely those of a disciplinarian and trainer.

Perhaps the put-downs of children are even worse. The list implies that these "ten commandments" are the most important things a five-year-old child should know and in no way urges his parents to teach him more.

Why doesn't the list say:

•If your child can read, it will benefit him greatly;

•If your child can already compute numbers to one hundred, it will help him to achieve;

•If your child can paint pictures, he will have a headstart;

• And why doesn't it say that he should be able to *write* his name, address, and telephone number and dial that number?

Don't these people who claim to be educators read anything except outdated curriculum guides? Why do they cling so tenaciously to the disputed theories of Rousseau, Gesell, and Piaget? Haven't they ever heard the names Doman, Bloom, Suzuki, Montessori, Kagan, and so on? Or do they think at all?

If these people are truly educators then why aren't they more interested in the education of the child? If they are teachers then why aren't they more interested in the learning of the child?

The First R—Reading

In the last two hundred years, the ability to read has been considered the necessary step in the development of the brighter child. The ability to read was believed to be the key to unlocking young minds and filling heads with the knowledge of Mankind.

Long before the term "reading readiness" was invented by the school people, it was believed that some children had the ability to pursue academic studies and others did not. The ones who showed an aptitude for academics were encouraged to become scholars; the others were left to dig ditches and play pool. Today, we feel the urgent need for all children to be educated. And to most people, "educated" means literate.

In this age of programmed reading readiness materials, the school systems readily admit that 30 percent of the grade-school children still do not read on grade level and 5 percent do not learn to read at all. While reading may not be the only skill presented to gradeschoolers, it is evident that mastery of the written word or failure to perceive it comprises a high percentage of the evaluative factors which determine their grades.

If a child meets the challenge and learns to read, then his chances of enjoying success in school are almost guaranteed.

But if your child falls within that 30 percent who do not read on grade level or has the misfortune to be a part of that 5 percent who are not learning to read at all, then you, as a parent, will be concerned about your child's ability to learn. Although his success as an individual in the adult world does not depend entirely upon being able to read literary journals or solve algebraic equations, parents are aware that his inability to do these things will decrease the choices of professions he might have, and pose threats to both his present and his future.

At this point, I could quote a file drawer of statistics relating the inability of students to read or poor readers with the problems of juvenile delinquency and school dropout. Although these are important statistics, and have direct implications toward the advantages of teaching children to read, we need not review them at length. Most of us are already cognizant of the fact that children who can read well tend to do well in school; children who do not read well tend to do poorly. Based on our own years of experience in the hallowed halls of brick and ivy, we quickly recall that the achievers were the better readers and that nonreaders were in trouble much of the time. Readers face success as a daily routine; nonreaders face failure.

During the last thirty years, much has been written about boys named "Johnny" and girls named "Janey" who can't read. Why can't Johnny read? Why can't Janey read? Why can't we teach them to read? We encounter very few dissertations asking why can't Johnny *hear* words and why can't Jane *speak* words? The reason is simple. Johnnys and Janeys have had the opportunity to hear and say words from the time they were born.

Most Johnnys and Janeys do not read words before coming to school because they have not had the opportunity to read words—or have they? How many preschoolers do you know who select their own cereal at the supermarket? How many preschoolers can read *Coke* and *Jello* and *Disneyland?* The fact is, in this televised, motor-dominated, jet-propelled age, preschool children are learning to read long before they are presented with reading readiness programs. If they learn these things at home on a catch-as-catch-can basis, why can't they learn to read at school? The answer to that is simpler than we might think. *Children are past their learning peaks by the time they enter school.*

Ever so slowly, the school people are catching on to this. We are now hearing murmurs suggesting that children should start to school *before* they are five years of age. I suspect those murmurs will grow louder daily, because such proposals are becoming more seductive to adults who work outside the home and to the school system's line of unemployed. Although herding children under five years of age inside the doors of school buildings might free parents of their care and provide more jobs for teachers, there is little evidence to indicate that such alternatives would benefit the children.

There are many misconceptions about what schools do and what they have done. If we listen to the school professionals we would be led to believe that *they* have brought literacy into the world and that without them the world would return to pictographs. Wrong again!

"Literacy has, in fact, always run well ahead of schooling," declares Everett Reimer in his book *School Is Dead.* "According to census data, there are always more literate members of a society than persons who have gone to schools. . . . In general, the children of literate parents learn to read even if they do not attend school, while the children of illiterate parents frequently fail to learn even in school."[2] So, it is more precise to conclude that parents, not schools, have increased the levels of literacy.

I have never understood why some teachers adamantly continue to defend the position that mothers should not teach their children to read before school age. If these teachers had read the statistics which clearly indicate that 30 percent of the children coming into school will have reading problems, I would think that upon finding those children who can already read that they would say, "Thank God, I'm not going to have to worry about them—they can already do it!" Instead they seem to resent the fact that a plain, ordinary mother, without blackboard or curriculum guide, has taught her child. It seems to annoy professionals when an amateur beats them at their own game.

Annoy them or not, I resent anyone even *imagining* that mothers are amateur teachers, for they are not. Motherhood is teaching personified (a principle we will explore in detail in a later chapter). At any rate, mothers by the tens of thousands around the world have proved beyond the shadow of a doubt that they can teach their preschoolers not only to read, but they have taught them languages, mathematics, geography, biology, sociology, psychology, and thousands of other related and unrelated pieces of information.

A big stumbling block has been that professionals have continued to consider that reading a written language is a school subject while hearing an auditory language and speaking a verbal language are natural processes. But it just isn't so. Lucky for the children, the school people haven't tried to stop mothers from teaching their children to hear and speak a language before they enter school. What a mess that would be!

In his book *How to Teach Your Baby to Read,* Glenn Doman removes reading as a subject from the curriculum guides, and places it where it properly belongs—in the brain:

> . . . Simply stated, and from a neurological standpoint, reading is not a school subject at all: It is a brain function.
>
> *Reading language is a brain function exactly as hearing language is a brain function.*
>
> What would our reaction be if, in examining a child's classroom subjects, we found geography, spelling, civics, and hearing?

Surely we would say, what is hearing doing there, listed as a school subject? Hearing is something the brain does, not to be confused with subjects taught in school.

So is reading.[3]

We have been gulled into believing that the written word is more difficult to perceive than is the spoken word. This simply is not true. ". . . don't you see, reading words is no different than hearing words," says Doman, "except hearing is done with the ears and reading is done with the eyes."[4]

Since learning to read has been erroneously considered an improbable feat for preschoolers, until recently, no one seemed to properly organize visual presentations for very young children. Even so, the youngsters' genius for assembling and sorting vast amounts of information prevailed, and they managed to make sense out of scattered fragments.

For instance—a child sees a collie and he says, "What's that?"

We say, "It's a dog."

A few days later he sees a Pekingese and says, "What's that?"

We say, "It's a dog."

Some time later, he sees a poodle and says, "What's that?"

And we say, "It's a dog."

During their first three or four years, children take such conglomerations of information and say, "All those things on four legs which look quite different from each other are dogs. And some of those things which don't look a lot different are sheep, and tigers, and lions." Yet soon, very young children understand which ones are dogs and which ones are the other things.

In most instances, before a child sees written words, he has already perceived the auditory sounds for those words, and is capable of giving each of them the correct verbal sounds. For example, the child has heard the word *cat* and he understands that the sound "cat" means a small animal with soft fur that goes, "meow." He is able to say the sound "cat," and when he says "cat," he knows that this sound will communicate to others that he is referring to a small animal with soft fur, long whiskers, pointed ears, and which walks on four feet and goes, "meow."

When the child is shown the written symbol, *cat,* he is not being introduced to a new word; he is being shown how that word, which he has heard many times and said many times, looks in print.

A new door has been unlocked for him. He is shown the secret of the written word. His life, at that moment, changes, and he will never again be the same. He has been given the key that allows him to pass into the world of Dr. Seuss, Mark Twain, Robert Louis Stevenson, Rudyard Kipling, and, eventually, Shakespeare.

Although over ten years ago Glenn Doman clearly demonstrated that children learn to read easier and better when the words are presented to them in large, clear print, we still see children's books printed in type so small that it makes one wonder if the publishers are trying to discourage future customers. Producers of televised teaching materials and the workbook publishers have fallen into the same rut. They present visual chaos rather than clear, easy-to-see illustrations and print. It's as if they're *daring* children to decipher the code and learn.

Worse still, they have built their material presentations upon the sinking sands of educational misconceptions and mistakes. The producers of television teaching programs for children have fallen into the same trap. I am appalled when I see a series of words flash across the television screen which are supposed to present a clear understanding of groups of words—*hand, hard, hot, hoot, head, hood.* What they are really doing is lining up a group of words which are extremely similar in appearance and defying the kids to tell them apart. It's crazy!

Obviously it is far simpler to discern the difference between the words *ostrich* and *hippopotamus* than it is to see the difference between the words *hoot* and *hood.* Yet time and time again presentations consist of words placed in nice, even rows, which look very much alike and sound very much alike. They are sometimes called "teacher's helpers," but no matter what they are termed, because of their similarities, they are nothing but learner's stumbling blocks.

No word should be considered too difficult simply because it is long. In fact, some of the longer words are easier to learn because of their unique appearances—such as *encyclopedia,* and *teeter-totter.* After hearing thousands of children, three and four years of age saying, *supercalifragilisticexpealidosious,* it should be unquestionably clear to us that children can learn to say any word we can give them. They can also learn to read any word if it is presented to them in a clear, uncluttered manner.

Adding insanity upon insanity, educators continue to purport that the beginning reader must "sound out" the words before he can learn to read them. Dumb! Dumb! Dumb!

A-ten-shun! The spelling of the word may not be acceptable, but, phonetically, it is readable and correct. "Sound it out, Johnny!" Johnny and Janey would gladly sound out words, and in little time might be able to read almost anything if it weren't for the inconsistent hurdles our language places before them. What child at his first encounter with *canoe* has not read it as *can-o-e,* or *coyote* as *coi-ot, bouquet* as *bow-ket,* and *cello* as *sel-o?*

If the rules were fixed, then perhaps the use of phonetics might increase the student's reading vocabulary. Perhaps. But they are not.

Small children, with their fast-growing, fast-learning brains, simply don't need all the "little helpers" dreamed up by slow, gray-haired old educators. If one were attempting to teach ninety-year-olds to read for the first time, one might need all the helpers he could get. But when teaching little kids, all that is needed is to *show* them the word and tell them what it is. The word goes into the memory bank of the marvelous computer brain in their heads.

Several years ago, a British publisher asked Glenn Doman to write a foreword to a book about teaching babies to read. When he read the book, he found that the author had fallen prey to the phonetic trap and had suggested that mothers heap mounds of verbal coughs and snorts upon the ears of their children. He wrote the following:

> I agree with virtually all, but not quite all, that Felicity Hughes has to say. My only disagreement with her comes in the area of phonetics and it is difficult for me to understand how so bright a girl, as she obviously is, could have fallen for that series of grunts, surds and sibilants called phonemes and morphemes from which the people called linguists have constructed an empire. I believe that Mrs. Hughes taught her children to read despite rather than because of phonetics. . . .[5]

Because Doman's book had been a runaway bestseller in the United Kingdom, and because he is considered the leading expert on the subject, and his name on the book would help sell copies, both the author and the publisher accepted the criticism and printed his statement intact.

Doman's method of teaching young children to read enjoys success for several reasons:

•The words are presented in large type-size.

•The total word is shown and the child is not confused by a thousand and one exceptions to the rules.

•The words are already familiar sounds to the child.

•They are presented during his early years when the child is capable of faster learning.

•No one tells the child that reading is any more complicated than looking at pictures or hearing words.

•The words are presented in the warm security of his home by a loving parent.

•It is easy.

•And it is fun.

In his book *How to Teach Your Baby to Read,* Doman offers the best list of reasons I have ever encountered for teaching children at an early age.

> The earlier a child reads, the more he is likely to read, and the better he reads.
>
> Some of the reasons, then, that children should learn to read when they are very young are as follows:
>
> *a.* The hyperactivity of the two- and three-year-old child is, in fact, the result of a boundless thirst of knowledge. If he is given an opportunity to quench that thirst, at least for a small part of the time, he will be far less hyperactive, far easier to protect from harm, and far better able to learn about the world when he is moving about and learning about the physical world and himself.
>
> *b.* The child's ability to take in information at two and three years of age will never be equaled again.
>
> *c.* It is infinitely easier to teach a child to read at this age than it will ever be again.
>
> *d.* Children taught to read at a very young age absorb a great deal *more information* than do children whose early attempts to learn are frustrated.
>
> *e.* Children who learn to read while very young tend to comprehend better than youngsters who do not. It is interesting to listen to the three-year-old who reads with inflection and meaning, in contrast to the average seven-year-old, who reads each word separately and without appreciation of the sentence as a whole.
>
> *f.* Children who learn to read while very young tend to read much more rapidly and comprehensively than children who do not. This is because young children are much less awed by reading and do not consider it a "subject" full of frightening abstractions. Tiny children view it as just another fascinating thing in a world jammed with fascinating things to be learned. They do not "hang up" on the details

but deal with reading in a totally functional sense. They are very right to do so.

g. Finally—and at least as important as the above stated reasons—children love to learn to read at a very early age.[6]

In literally all parts of the world today, mothers are teaching their preschoolers to read. They are not pushing or coercing their children into doing something that is difficult. Instead, they are showing them how simple learning to read can be and how much fun it is to use the code.

In her article "A Happy Headstart in Reading," Shirley Carter writes:

Our four-and-a-half-year-old daughter enthusiastically mastered beginning reading skills in about five months. Now in kindergarten, she is reading at second-grade level. Should I have followed the advice of the many educators who believe in a hands-off policy for parents, for fear of the mistakes they may make in teaching their children to read? . . .

On the basis of my own happy experience, I feel that parents can help a child who wants to read. Surely no one will ever know your child better than you do in these preschool years—his interests, likes and dislikes, vocabulary and capabilities. . . . parents don't have to be experts to help them when they show a real desire to learn to read. So why not give your own interested youngster a head start? It is an absorbing and rewarding experience for parent and child alike.[7]

If you have a bright and alert preschooler, you will be surprised at how quickly he or she will learn.

During the same time our eight-year-old son was on the programs of therapy, Nancy was also teaching him to read. Our daughter, Traci, who was four years old, watched from the sidelines. One morning Nancy held up a card before

Todd with the word *hand* printed on it. Before Todd could answer, Traci said, "I know that word."

Nancy turned to her and asked, "What is it?"

Traci answered correctly.

In a matter of minutes, Nancy found that Traci knew all the words that had been presented to Todd. So, the reading lessons became a class for two. Soon Traci knew all the words on all the cards. She began reading books and became so proficient that some mornings she would show Todd the word cards and correct him when his answers were wrong. Within a year, she had read *Lassie, Come Home, The Yearling,* and several of the Laura Ingalls Wilder "Little House" books, and was perusing articles in *Life, Look,* and other periodicals.

While Todd's was a planned program, Traci seemed to learn by osmosis.

How soon should you begin to teach your baby to read?

As soon as he is ready.

How soon will he be ready to learn?

Probably sooner than you are ready to teach him.

If he is four years old, run, don't walk.

If he is three years old, you've already missed the prime time.

If he's two, don't wait.

If he's one year old, you have a head start on a lot of other mothers, but you might have started sooner.

You will find that it's fun, it's easier than you think, and it doesn't take hours and hours—probably fifteen minutes a day will do the trick.

If you are ready to begin, I recommend that you purchase *The Doman Reading Kit.* It is complete with all the materials you will need, and contains easy-to-follow instructions. Although you can make many of the materials yourself, that is time-consuming and there is the possibility that for the want of a new-lettered card, you might slow the progress of your child's learning.

On some days, you will find that your child may learn only

one or two words and is ready to stop, or that his attention is diverted to something else. When that happens, move on to something else. However, that exciting day will arrive when everything clicks and he will learn fifteen or twenty words as quickly as you can show them to him. If you have printed only five cards, he has just been cheated out of ten additional words, and you have lost a marvelous experience.

The kit costs about ten dollars and I believe you will find that it is money well spent. If you have more than one child, one kit is still all you need. After you have finished with it, sell it to a neighbor or a friend, or, if you feel generous, give it to them.

The kit should be available at all bookstores. However, if you have difficulty finding it, you can order one from The Institutes bookstore:

The Doman Reading Kit
The Book Store
The Institutes for the Achievement of Human Potential
8801 Stenton Avenue
Philadelphia, Pennsylvania 19118

The Second R—'Rithmetic

Several times in this writing it has been mentioned that mothers not only can, but do, teach their preschoolers such diverse subjects as language, mathematics, biology, sociology, psychology, and so on. I'm sure this statement would cause many educators to shout frantically, "This man is a lunatic!" But that would have nothing to do with whether the lunatic is right or not. It would only reflect their lack of understanding of what the lunatic is saying. Whether they understand or not has very little to do with how mothers function as teachers or with the subject matter they teach. Mothers do better than teach subjects by category; they relate information within the child's experiences. Mothers teach *functional* mathematics, *functional* language, *func-*

tional biology, *functional* sociology, *functional* psychology, and so on.

Glenn Doman's name has frequently appeared in this writing and his philosophies and attitudes have appeared even more often. And rightfully so. His doctrine of early learning has been the major impetus in changing attitudes toward the potentials and abilities of children. One might say that he is the head of the children's liberation movement.

One day he said to me, "All mothers teach their children geography."

"How's that?" I asked.

"To a baby, his surroundings are the map of his world. The bedroom is the eastern terrain of the house. The living room is like another country. The floor is the flatland, and the sofa to any baby must appear as high as a mountain does to adults. Any mother who shows her baby his surroundings is giving him his first lessons in geography.

"When she takes him to a friend's house or when she has friends visit, she's teaching him sociology by example. By her actions, she is saying, 'Hey, kid, this is how people interract with one another.' How she deals with him and with other people sets a pattern of psychology. And obviously she teaches him a language, and mathematics, and all those beginning things.

"If a school teacher taught her class half as much in one year as a mother teaches her baby during the course of a month, the teacher would want a gold medal stuck on her chest. Yet, a mother expects no reward. Just seeing her child learn and grow is enough. Mothers are great people—especially for kids."

Teaching mathematics to a preschooler isn't difficult at all —in one form or another most mothers do it. If they realized how important it is for the child and how easily they can add to his knowledge, they would do even more. Who says mathematics has to be taught out of a book filled with dreary questions about the amount of milk Farmer Jones's cows produce? Or if Mary Brown has five dresses and she buys two new ones, how many dresses will Mary Jones have? Who cares?

When a mother shows her child that one object is larger than another she is teaching comparative sizes. Isn't that a basic math concept?

When a mother points out that one person or thing is taller than another she repeats this idea. Aren't taller and shorter the basics of measurement?

When a mother says, "Look, you have four blue blocks," isn't she teaching computation?

And when she says, "You have two red ones," isn't that sorting like kinds? Of course it is.

In the course of the everyday, mothers teach their kids mathematical concepts all the time. And so do fathers.

It is a hundred times better to teach in terms of the child's immediate personal surroundings than in terms of remote impersonal items about which the child could care less.

When a mother takes the extra time to show her child how she mixes a cake batter—four cups of flour, one and one-half cups of sugar, one cup of milk, one-half teaspoon vanilla, and so on, she is teaching a superb mathematics lesson—both measurement and computation. Mothers who become fully aware of this give their children a terrific head start.

Although I had no idea that it had anything to do with mathematics, before I was five years old I could count to one hundred. I could sort pennies into tens. I knew that ten dimes made a dollar, and that four quarters did too. And as far as I knew I had never had a lesson.

At the time, my father operated a string of ice routes. When he arrived home each evening, he sorted his change and wrapped the coins in paper wrappers so he could exchange them at the bank for paper currency. I thought the sorting and wrapping looked like great fun and I loved to help him. I'm sure my help often slowed the process, but he never let me know it.

In today's society, children often lack opportunities to relate the use of money to everyday events. When I was five years old, my mother sent me on errands to the corner grocery. My tip was usually a few pennies. (In those days one could buy things with pennies.) I learned what groceries cost and how to count the change. The problem today is that we write checks for almost everything or use credit cards. I imagine that it is all very confusing to children. One sack of groceries costs one check. And a television set costs one credit card.

And corner groceries are almost nonexistent except in inner cities where children should not be walking alone. What has happened is that we have created environments where children must have a grown protector or a chauffeur with them at all times.

However, mothers and fathers who are considerate enough during shopping expeditions, and allow their children to shop for items and pay for them, soon see their kids handling money with the ease of Swiss bankers. Too often, though, children are simply allowed to pick out something they want and the parents pick up the tab. Other than finding that Mom or Dad are generous, the children have learned almost nothing. On the other hand, if your child has a set amount of money in his pocket and has to make his choice of purchase accordingly, he can begin to gain a sense of pricing and monetary value.

"I want this one," he says.

"Yes, that is nice, but it costs sixty-five cents and you have only fifty. You can either choose something that costs fifty cents, or less, or save your money until you get more. Then you can come back and buy this."

It's a very simple lesson in economics. A child doesn't have to be six years old to learn such lessons. Letting his money be the determining factor in what he buys also takes pressure off the parents. If a child thinks that the determining factor in what he gets depends entirely on the mood of his parents, then it's difficult for him to understand why he can't have whatever he wishes. Of course there are times when he will see something "really special" and his parents have every right to say, "I'll give you another fifteen cents and then you'll have enough to buy it." Either way, he learns comparative shopping.

It's almost impossible for your child to go shopping without learning something. He can either learn that he must follow you like a puppy at all times, or he can learn that if he remains patient while you are shopping, he will soon be allowed to have his turn.

While observing you as you ask questions of the clerks, he learns the accepted bartering system and also learns attitudes. As soon as possible, allow him to ask his own questions and to pay the clerk. Most clerks are happy to spend the extra time with a child, or they certainly should be. Even an uncooperative clerk can be a learning experience for your child.

Should a clerk give your child an impatient sigh or try to hurry him, speak to her in cheerful, friendly tones (that's called psychology); if she is rude, remind her that she is paid to wait on customers no matter what their age (that's called sociology); if she persists in her disgust, tell the manager (that's called behavioral modification); if he doesn't alter either the clerk's disposition or hire a new clerk, never shop there again (that's called revenge). See how much your child might learn on one short shopping trip?

There are many games which help teach mathematical skills: Parcheesi, checkers, Monopoly, and almost any game that uses dice or a spinning wheel. However, dice and dominoes are better because the child has to compute the combinations. But the best way to teach a child how to play a game is for him to watch adults play it. First of all, if he sees that the big people enoy it, he'll be bursting at the seams with eagerness to try his hand. Don't show that you are eager to let him enter in. Wait until his curiosity is at its peak. And don't select the cutesy kids' games where chance is the major factor in winning. Get those that take some thought and planning.

There are thousands of opportunities to teach your child mathematics. Be inventive and use them. Your child's quickness in grasping the concepts will amaze you. And you'll become such an efficient teacher that you will surprise yourself.

A word of caution—don't become test happy. Don't continually make your child repeat and repeat and repeat the things he already knows. When you see that he has the idea —counting blocks, for instance—find other things for him to count. Always lead him on to new discoveries. Don't allow him to become tired of the old ones. Remember, he can learn rapidly, and once he has learned, he is ready to move on to other things. The real challenge is to your inventiveness and your ability to keep one step ahead of his interests and enthusiasm. One thing for sure, *you* may grow tired, and *you* may run out of energy, but if you stay one step ahead of an eager three-year-old you will never find time to be bored.

The Third R—'Riting

If you teach your child to read, you'll have no trouble teaching him to write. In fact, you'll have a difficult time trying to keep him from it—on paper, on walls, on sidewalks, on windows, the floor, the table, the living room sofa—any place he can reach for or climb to.

To save furniture from American graffiti, you might be wise to channel his urge to communicate. From the very beginning, show him that adults write on paper. Show him how to write his name. All kids love to write their own names.

At first do most of the writing yourself. Let him know that it is something that grownups can do and enjoy doing. If you are teaching him to read with the materials of *The Doman Reading Kit,* write all words the same size as those he is reading. Again, don't be too eager to turn the felt tip or the crayon or whatever you are using over to him. By intuition, you will know when he has the idea and is at the peak of his eagerness.

The first time he writes a word, show an animated response of both surprise and pride. Make him aware that you realize what a hero he is. Mothers are great at this. And kids truly love it!

Most important, if you show that you enjoy seeing your child learn new things, he'll enjoy learning them. What a nice way to grow his brain.

Someone Answer the Phone

With so many recognizing the importance of mothers and how they can alter their children's lives, one would think that all our problems in teaching children could be easily solved. All we would have to do is reach mothers and tell them the marvelous news.

Not long after I began this writing, a friend asked me what I was working on.

As an answer, he received a thirty-minute oration on the subject. When I paused for breath, my friend said, "All of this may be well and good, but do you think it will really make any difference?"

"What do you mean?" I asked.

"Do you think that if you tell mothers about these things they will actually *do* anything about it?"

"Sure I do," I answered. "Don't you?"

He took a sip of his favorite drink and replied, "I doubt it. If we called all the mothers in the country today, and told them this marvelous news, that by taking only a few minutes out of their day, they could accelerate their children's development, I can predict what we would find."

"What would we find?" I asked.

"If we phoned right now," he said, "we would find that over forty percent of the mothers aren't home—they're at work.

"Five percent won't answer the phone during their favorite soap opera or television game show.

"Another five percent are at a neighbor's gulping morning

coffee and sharing juicy tidbits of gossip about a mutual friend or potential enemy.

"Three percent are attending a woman's luncheon or anticipating an afternoon cocktail party.

"One percent won't be able to understand what we're saying because they couldn't wait for the cocktail party so they started on a bottle of their own.

"Four percent are in session with their analyst.

"Two percent will listen to the news and ask if they teach their child, will they be rewarded with a new dishwasher or an all-expense-paid trip to Hawaii for two.

"Ten percent say they are glad to hear the news and they'll think it over while they're at the hairdresser's.

"Two percent have unlisted numbers, so we won't be able to call them."

"Does that add up to one hundred percent?" I asked.

"I don't know. I lost track," he smiled. "Anyway, at most, maybe some small fraction of one percent will hang up the phone and start teaching their kids."

He poured himself another glass of scotch.

His comments greatly disturbed me. If what he said is true, the twentieth century has turned a large majority of mothers into displaced persons. What undeserving victims they are. It's even worse for the children.

Perhaps even good news can arrive too late, but for the sake of the children, let's hope it hasn't.

Chapter 5

The Purpose of Childhood— The Reason for Parents

"Look What They've Done To Your Song, Ma!"

The child is a slave to his environment. His nervous system develops by use. . . . A happy home, with loving parents who encourage him to learn, is an example of an excellent neurological environment. Playpens, institutions, and other cages are examples of poor neurological environments.

—RAYMUNDO VERAS, M.D.
Children of Dreams—Children of Hope[1]

If a mother is asked what she wants for her child, no matter where she lives or what station of life she has acquired, she will answer that she wants life to be better for him. Better than what? Better than life has been for her; better than life has been for his father; better. Better, of course, is a word or a condition which must have a comparison before it has true meaning. But we know what she means even if we do not know the conditions of her life. She wants more for her child. Perhaps it is our hopes for our children's future that constitute the most unselfish thoughts we ever have as human beings.

As you have probably realized long before now, these pages are not simply filled with pieces of information and statistics, but they also contain discussions of attitudes. I think we have come to a time in history when explorations of attitudes are just as important as are explorations of information and statistical evidence.

Unless numbers and facts are related to the everyday world of everyday people, then they become unrelated and forgotten data. What do I care that three to five billion dollars are going to be spent on school buildings during the next year? I have no idea what three to five billion dollars looks like. I don't know if it could be transported in a little red wagon or if it would fill the bed of a construction truck. What do you care if 30 percent of the children in this country read below grade level? If 30 percent of the children in this country lined up twelve abreast, how many miles would those lines extend? Who knows? Who cares? Those are the kinds of questions we would expect to find in an old-new-fun-and-games math book. Only accountants and stock brokers are interested in curved graph lines and percentage points.

As interested as parents may be about the welfare of *all* the children of the world, they do not really care nearly as much about *all* children as they do about their own. That should not surprise anyone. Nor should anyone disagree. Nor is there any reason for that situation to be changed.

We become interested in reading problems if one of *our* children has a reading problem, the same way we become interested in mumps if one of *our* children has swollen jaws. We are not as interested in how *all* children are taught and what *all* children are taught as we are in how and what our *own* children learn. That is not called selfishness; it is called survival.

It would be possible to discuss children without the mention of parents, but I hardly think it would be profitable, because both the presence and the absense of parents greatly affect the lives of children.

Our decisions in regard to how and what our children are going to learn in the future will affect the lives of both children and parents.

As you have probably guessed, I like mothers and I have

a great deal of respect for motherhood. I think a mother and a child make a great team. So, let's first take a look at what's happening to mothers in particular, and motherhood in general.

Slings and Arrows of Outrageous Fortune

In recent years, there have been many articles similar to the one entitled "Motherhood: Who Needs It?" which appeared in *Look.* "Motherhood is in trouble, and it ought to be," writes Betty Rollin, *Look* senior editor. "A rude question is long overdue: Who needs it? The answer used to be 1) society and 2) women." And she continues to state:

> The notion that the maternal wish and the activity of mothering are instinctive or biologically predestined is baloney. Try asking most sociologists, psychologists, psychoanalysts, biologists—many of whom are mothers —about motherhood being instinctive; it's like asking department-store presidents if their Santa Clauses are real. "Motherhood—instinctive?" shouts distinguished sociologist/author, Dr. Jessie Bernars. "Biological destiny? Forget biology! If it were biology, people would die from not doing it."
>
> ". . . There are no instincts," says Dr. William Goode, president-elect of the American Sociological Association. "There are reflexes, like eye-blinking, and drives, like sex. There is no innate drive for children. Otherwise, the enormous cultural pressures that there are to reproduce wouldn't exist. There are no cultural pressures to sell you on getting your hand out of the fire."[2]

These types of articles are flashy and often entertaining, but it would be difficult to call them either accurate or reasonable. They often start with truths, enter into half-truths, and then gallop into wild conjectures. I do not mind wild conjectures and am prone to enter into them myself, but I would be totally reluctant to present half-truths as truths and conjectures as facts.

Look was one of the first popular magazines to feature such an attack on motherhood. While the magazine was in its waning years, others that would embrace such philosophies, such as *Ms.,* were being conceived, and many home-oriented periodicals were soon to be altered to champion the cause of the liberated woman. A new style was being set. By 1976, attacks on motherhood are more numerous and stronger, while articles defending its virtues are fewer and weaker. In the August 1975 issue of *Ladies' Home Journal,* the following letter from a reader was published:

> Hey, *Journal,* I thought you were catching up with the times. Then comes that sentimental fashion story called, "To Mother with Love." I know these were models with their own children, but stop promoting motherhood all the time. We have other options now, remember?[3]

The *Journal*'s editors responded, "Yes, we remember," and referred the reader to an article in the current issue that emphasized how financially costly having children can be.

Women may have come a long way, but where are they going?

But Muskrats Don't Know Any Better

It is easy to agree that the longing to become a mother is not a biological drive, and we can agree that nothing biologically bad happens to women if they do not become mothers. For instance, they don't sprout hair on their lips or warts on their earlobes. Obviously, many women lead full and rewarding lives without becoming mothers.

It is apparent that the female muskrat does not flirt with the male muskrat in order to have babies. Her biological drive is not to become a mother, just as the male muskrat's biological drive is not to become a father. Their biological drives are for a quick tumble in the grass. Happily, for all the little muskrats, the male and female have no idea that the romp on the green is going to result in a litter of responsibilities—if they did, perhaps they would have as many neuroses as male and female people.

Sex may be the reason for the reproduction of the species, but the sexual drive has little to do with the desire for children. If the only reason for two people to engage in sexual intercourse was to have children, there would be many cold winter nights. Sex is a biologically pleasurable act. Since the pleasure derived from it can often provide us with more children than we can financially or emotionally care for, it is clear why we devise contraceptive measures rather than abstain from this biological urge. So strongly does sex influence our lives that we feel its effects physically, emotionally, and even develop fantasies about it.

While to become a mother or a father is not a biological drive, once a woman becomes a mother, it would be foolish for us to deny that she does have biological instincts in caring for that child and that those instincts are far stronger than are those of the male. To deny that would be like denying that trees have leaves. After all, a mother has carried her child within her body—she has given birth to it—and her body contains the child's primary food supply unit. It would be pure fantasy for us to conjecture that men have the potential of becoming as good mothers as women do.

I would not argue for a moment that the woman's role in caring for small children places a greater responsibility upon her. In a purely biological sense, she often pays a higher price for her sexual and emotional attachments.

Despite what we have been told in romantic novels, it is doubtful that many people marry for the prime purpose of conceiving children. They marry in order to live together.

Children are a by-product of that togetherness.

Today there is an enormous problem confronting parents of preschoolers. In some cases it touches fathers, but for the most part, it reaches out with clenched fists and holds mothers. It can be called all kinds of things. It is a social problem. It is often an economic problem. It can also be termed a statistical problem. It is certainly a personal problem. And it is one, I must admit from the beginning, that I cannot solve for you. Even if I could, I'm not sure I should attempt to interfere.

Many women are chorusing in voices loud and clear that the old days of woman's servitude to husband and family are gone. They feel that a full-time role of housewife and mother robs them of their own identity and cheats them of opportunities to have successful careers. A large number of women feel that during the years when their children are small and so dependent they, as individuals, are forced to endure a period of confinement and isolation from the mainstream of life.

There are those who maintain that the father should share equally in the responsibilities of rearing the children, and that married couples should share fifty-fifty in both careers and home duties. Some couples have managed to blend the two successfully, but many others wind up yelling at one another in divorce courts.

I was not born a male chauvinist pig, but I'm sure that many of those sociological standards have inflicted and infected my attitudes. Still, as a human being who is smitten with the urge to be both an individual and creative, I must admit, and better still, reckon with, human needs and human concerns—whether they be male or female.

I see in my own wife a bright and attractive person—a well-read, well-informed human being by anyone's standards. I vividly remember her during the years when our children were little and so demanding of her time. I know there were times when she felt like a caged animal, longing desperately to have a conversation with another adult about anything other than the problems of potty training and vaccination schedules.

I look at our daughter, Traci, and see in her an extremely creative and talented individual with an enormous range of potential. Professionally, I'm sure she could excel in any career she might choose. I think she could become a doctor, a lawyer, an actress, or a singer, and she writes with an ease of poetic fluidity and maturity far beyond what is expected of a sixteen-year-old. Unless she makes a rare find, I'm not sure that the man she might choose will be either as bright, as intelligent, or as creative as she. I'm not sure but what I would resent some hunk of muscled beefyness restricting her energies to the routine of daily housework. So I find that I have become schizophrenic in regard to this subject.

There are those who will argue that housework and raising children demand as much creativity and bring as many rewards as does a career. However, I have noticed that those who offer such opinions are usually men who don't know a dust mop from a vacuum sweeper, or which end of a baby should be diapered or burped.

Perhaps the best word for housework is monotony. Drudgery is another good one. "If I have to pick up one more pair of socks, I think I'll start screaming and never stop!" The best words for motherhood are time-consuming, patience, and perserverence. "Tommy tried to flush his teddy bear down the stool today."

But call it drudgery, call it perserverence, or whatever it may be labeled or libeled, both housework and motherhood are basic essentials.

Although there are parents who are guilty of neglecting and ignoring their children, I've found these people to be in the minority. They are parents only by definition; they are actually progenitors. Legally, they may be guardians, but they are not caring protectors. Fortunately, they are rarely in charge of large numbers of children due to biological limitations. I admit that there are insensitive parents. I admit that there are ignorant parents. And I admit that there are stupid parents. I admit it. I do. But these people are not simply insensitive, ignorant, stupid parents; they are insensitive, ignorant, stupid people who happen to be parents.

Now that I have admitted their existence, let's not discuss this minority at any greater length. I am assuming that the readers of this material have this book because they are interested in the futures of their children, and are concerned about the direction and the influence they have on their children's lives.

There are those who maintain that life in the past was simpler because the roles of adulthood were better defined. I don't believe that. The roles may have been defined, but it is doubtful that they were better because they were so limiting. Limiting people to fixed and unquestionable stations in society is neat and orderly, but rarely is it just or even humane.

Nevertheless, we have the responsibility to insure that our children's welfare takes top priority. If the needs of the children confront the wants and wishes of the adults—that's tough! As parents, Nancy and I have had to deal with these problems. As parents, you do too. Sometimes we have dealt with them honestly and even courageously; sometimes our solutions have been selfish and even foolish. In complete honesty, I can say that Nancy has consistently been a better mother than I have been a father. And just as honestly, she will agree to that. But that doesn't mean that that's the way it should be.

Today, a good number of men are becoming more aware of women's dilemmas and are getting over the nonsense that washing dishes or running the vacuum are threats to their masculinity. The smarter men caught on to this sooner than the duller ones.

However, if we are concerned with what is best for our children, we cannot blithely ignore biological qualifications and millions of years of built-in genetic instincts. It would be difficult, if not impossible, for us to conclude anything other than, biologically, females have more potential to be mothers than do men. Not only in giving birth and functioning as a milk factory, but they also have the biological desire. How many of their instincts are genetic rather than programmed by their early years may be debatable, but without a doubt, historically, they have been the child rearers. To assume or even dream that men, in large numbers, will willingly or by force (either emotional or social) take over the rearing of children would be out and out fantasy. It simply will not occur in our lifetime, and it is highly questionable that the twenty-first or the twenty-second centuries will bring about such drastic changes.

The real and immediate threat to our children is female desertion—the removal of women from the role of mother, which will eventually require placing youngsters in day-care centers. On a wide scale, this is already happening by the tens of thousands. While it is purported that such centers free women to pursue careers or, by necessity, to earn an income, there is practically no indication that those places provide even a second-rate substitute for an inventive and loving mother.

While I could go on and on about the injustice to the female as an individual and how having children alters and even limits her personal aspirations, that is not the purpose of this book. The purpose of this book is to discuss what is best for children once they have been conceived and delivered into this world. If in the course of this discussion we find that what is best for children conflicts with the personal ambition of the parents, then I have no choice but to defend the children.

Whether or not adults find these attitudes and actions detrimental to the development of children, many adults will probably still do as they damned well please. They usually do, but those are their decisions to make. I do not wish to set myself up as the conscience of all adults—just as I would not want others to become my conscience. If adults are aware of how children are abused and neglected and choose to go on their merry way, that is their business. But I do not want to be subjected to nonsensical excuses and unreasonable rationalizations.

Don't tell me that it makes no difference how children are cared for.

Don't tell me that it makes no difference what children are taught.

Don't tell me that it makes no difference if children are herded together like cattle.

If you do, I shall tell you that Columbus sailed off the edge of the earth, that storks bring babies, and that Burt Reynolds is really Henry Kissinger in disguise.

The Choreography of Mother and Baby

It appears that the proponents of the Women's Liberation Movement, in their struggle for equality, forget or neglect to relate a vast number of opinions and facts pertaining to the mother-child relationship if those opinions and facts are in opposition to their cause. In order to claim that mothers do not need children and that children do not need mothers, and that the two are better if separated, they have to ignore a mountain of scientific and empirical evidence.

"The relation between infant and mother is a ballet, in which each partner responds to the steps of the other," observes Jerome Kagan in his article "His Struggle for Identity." "If, when the infant cries, the mother bestows care and affection, the infant will be likely to cry on the next occasion when he is distressed. Thus the mother's actions are molding the infant's behavior."[4]

". . . We are just beginning to appreciate the critical role the mother plays in language development," stresses Charles E. Silberman in his book *Crisis in the Classroom.* ". . . Middle-class children's greater facility with language is the product, in large part, of the fact that middle-class mothers have more time for reciprocal play with their children than do lower-class mothers. In a sense, teachers in formal classrooms do consciously and deliberately what mothers do unconsciously and more or less instinctively."[5]

"By the time the baby is a year old, the mother and baby will have a pattern of dealing with each other that reveals to an observant onlooker . . . the promise of a healthy or unhealthy relationship," reports Vivian Cadden in her article " 'Yes' to Love and Joyful Faces." ". . . It is of enormous importance that the community . . . help them understand the ways in which the baby's development unfolds and, if need be, actually to help them with the care of the baby."[6]

And T. Berry Brazelton, M.D., asserts that a mother functions as a secure base for her infant's initial explorations, and without her presence, a baby takes far less interest in his environment.

"By repeatedly noticing and responding to his wants, needs and expectations," Dr. Brazelton says, "a mother gives her baby the pleasure of being the cause—of learning how to act in order to produce the results he wants, of learning about things that are the results of his own actions. Here is real learning! It takes place with great rapidity, it is dependent largely upon the mother. . . . She must stand between her baby and his world, interpreting, patient, and sensitive. This is true mothering."[7]

Mothers analyze the potential of their children. How many mothers have you heard introduce their sons as future doctors, engineers, mechanics, or even future Presidents of the United States? A mother may introduce her daughter as a future singer, dancer, or teacher. If you think she is joking, you have not looked into her eyes. Mothers are deadly serious about the futures of their children, and one has only to look at the people who have succeeded in becoming doctors, lawyers, singers, teachers, and, yes, even Presidents of the United States, to realize how many mothers have achieved their goals.

It may appear that because I place so much emphasis on the mother-child relationship, I have given little importance to the father-child relationship. That has not been my intention. Men who gleefully leave this responsibility of raising children to their wives, and those who feel justified in walking away from family responsibility would do well to reappraise what effects their absense can have upon their offspring.

"Children from father-absent homes, at least initially, are more submissive, dependent, effeminate, and susceptible to group influence," report Urie Bronfenbrenner and John Condry, Jr., in their book *Two Worlds of Childhood: U.S. and U.S.S.R.* ". . . Thus in lower-class Negro families, where father absence is particularly common, the typically passive and dependent boy readily transfers his attachment to the gang, where, to earn and keep his place, he must demonstrate his toughness and aggressiveness.[8]

If we were going to set out to propose the ultimate situation in which children can be raised, we would likely conclude that every child should have a "Father Knows Best" family. The father comes home from the office in his neatly pressed suit and is met at the door by his adoring wife. Her apron is spotless and she appears as if she has just stepped out of the hairdresser's instead of the kitchen. During the day she has more than enough time to attend to the needs of her children. The washer never breaks down. The house never needs a new coat of paint. Bill collectors never call. The bank account is never overdrawn. Both parents listen to their children's problems, which are always minor. "Tommy never puts the soap back in the tray" or "Sandra Wilson is having a party and she didn't invite me." All problems can be and are solved in thirty minutes, minus commercials. Such existence is a fantasy—a lovely, entertaining fantasy, but a fantasy all the same. But wouldn't it be lovely for the kids?

Of course there should be a few fringe benefits for the children. Every backyard would have its own oak tree supporting a rope swing and a treehouse. The driveway would be marked by roller skate wheels. Every neighborhood would have at least one bonafide haunted house. And within a ten-minute walk, there would be a swimming hole fed by a brook teaming with trout.

Such dreams are miles and decades from the sidewalks of New York and the concrete apartment buildings of Chicago. They are lost from the suburbs of Kansas City and Dallas and Cleveland. They have been swallowed up by developers of condominiums and rows of housing projects.

Today we are faced with air pollution, the energy crisis, inflation, and recession—not one at a time, but all together. However, I'm not one to walk around moaning that all is lost, because I don't think all is lost. If I had a choice of today's woes or the past plagued with scarlet fever and poliomyelitis, I would take the problems confronting us now rather than in any other period in history.

We know more about ourselves today and we have the time to be more creative and productive than ever before. At the same time, we must set priorities. Heading our list of priorities must be the proper care of our children.

The purpose of childhood is to introduce the new members of our species to their environment so they can learn its social order, become acquainted with physical and emotional dangers, and be made aware of opportunities and choices. The reason for parents is to provide those learning experiences for their children.

If you were the parent of a child in a primitive society, you would introduce him to a village of grass huts and jungle surroundings. You would teach him the rank and file of the tribe. You would caution him about snakes and wild beasts, and protect him in the darkness of night. You would teach him to throw a spear and how to catch a fish. You would instill in him those attitudes and skills which would be expected of him as an adult in his society.

In our culture, parents introduce their children to cities of brick and concrete. They caution them about traffic in the streets, show them how to obey signals, and how to buy food at the supermarket. Parents teach their children to be courteous to others and to obey the law of the land. And since, in our society, words have become both our means of friendly discourse and our ultimate weapons, we should teach our children how to use them from a very early age. The better the individual's command and understanding of language and the social structure in which he is born, the more choices he has in his life. It is only when people are at a loss for words that they revert to hurling spears, shooting bullets, and throwing grenades.

Gone from Nine to Five

Parenthood isn't an easy task, even when both mother and father are functioning partners. It's next to impossible for one person to try to fufill both roles. Being a mother, responsible for the welfare of her children, without a father to share that responsibility is more to ask of a woman than should be asked. Still there are many women who have to take on that task alone. It is unfair and it is unjust. Since most of these women have to maintain a job to help provide or completely provide for their families, it is an added insult that they are most often paid lesser salaries than are their male counterparts. So often these mothers must leave their children in the care of others, and there is a great need for proper places for these children where they can receive the love and the stimulation needed for their growth.

There are those who argue that quality time with children is better than quantity time. These people assert that some working mothers spend more productive time with their children than do other mothers who stay home. I'm sure that this is true. And isn't it a shame. But what mothers are they really comparing. Aren't they comparing working mothers who purposefully put forth such efforts with nonworking mothers who do not? Is it possible for a working mother, even though she is conscientious, to match the efforts of a nonworking mother who really tries? It is doubtful, indeed.

One of the most important factors in teaching young children is catching them when their interest is at its peak. That peak time can be manipulated and it can be encouraged, but it is highly questionable whether it can be scheduled to only those hours when the mother is home from work. By the end of this book, it should be evident that teaching a preschooler does not require hours on end, but it often requires minutes utilized out of the course of hours. It is highly advantageous for a mother to be on hand when the child is ready to learn rather than expect the child to adapt to the mother's schedule.

Am I saying that mothers who work should not try to accelerate their children's abilities? I certainly am not! What I am saying is that they are handicapped with the penalties of time and energy limitations. And so is the child. These mothers and children need all the help they can get. Dad may have to chip in and become a part-time mother. And the babysitter may find that she needs to turn off the soap operas and tend to more than the child's meals, baths, and naptimes.

If you are a working mother, you might be well advised to see that your child's sitter (whether it's Dad, or Aunt Sally, or the woman down the street) reads this book and realizes how important that job is.

If you are a working mother, I wish you the very best of luck.

If you are a nonworking mother, how very lucky you are. I hope you make the best of your time. If you do, both you and your child are in for many exciting adventures.

Chapter 6

Everyone Knows That Some Children Are Geniuses, Some Children Are Gifted, Some Are Bright and Alert, Some Are Average, and Some Are Genetic Duds

---

Who Says?

Take a look at the following news items:

Princeton, West Virginia

Norman Platnick, at sixteen, has been accepted as a teaching fellow at Michigan State University. Norman entered Concord, West Virginia, College when he was in the seventh grade. He finished *World Book Encyclopedia* in second grade.

Fayette, Alabama

Michael Shepherd's kindergarten teacher has a shock in store when he enters Fayette Kindergarten, Monday morning. Michael can already read, write, spell, and work arithmetic problems.

Moorhead City, North Carolina

Kenneth Fischler, a fifth grader at Camp Glenn School, has been selected to attend special education classes for intellectually gifted students at Western Carolina University this summer.

Salem, Oregon

Bruce Bengston, Salem's gifted fourteen-year-old organist, now on a concert tour in Europe, is being widely acclaimed.

Salem, Ohio

The report that a fifteen-year-old Filipino girl, Maria Teresa Calderon, can read 5,000 words a minute with nearly 100 percent comprehension taxes the credulity of most of us.

Maria's ability to scan, absorb, and comprehend rivals that of today's computers. One cannot help but marvel at the capacity of the human brain and its potential for development and/or improvement.

Waukegan, Illinois

At the age of fifteen, Phillip Youderian has entered Williams College, Williamstown, Massachusetts, as a freshman with advanced placement in mathematics and organic chemistry.

India

Manoj Kuman Prasad of India, enters the University of Florida next week at age thirteen, the youngest student ever recorded at the university.

Manoj speaks Spanish, Hindi, and English fluently. He is intent on a physics degree, following in the footsteps of both his parents and a grandfather.

His father, Dr. Sheo Shanker Prasad, is an associate professor at the university.

Kansas, Illinois

A twelve-year-old boy, whose "mind is like a blotter," has enrolled as a freshman at City College in New

York. Such developments always exert a particular fascination on those of us whose minds, far from soaking up knowledge like a blotter, often seem stubbornly impervious to it.

Matthew Marcus is, by any standard, a most uncommon sort of boy. He learned to read at age four and now, at a time when most children are entering junior high school, is launched on a course of study that includes advanced calculus and honors courses in English and physics.

Opelousas, Louisiana

By special permission of the State Department of Education, Mary Foster, a third-year student at Morrow High School, will receive her high school diploma after six more weeks of study. Miss Foster has maintained a perfect 4.0 record in all her studies at Morrow High.

I have hundreds of such news articles in my files. What do these stories mean? Do they mean that there are more freak geniuses in the world? Or do they mean that parents are catching on to the fact that young children have untapped genius and they have already begun tapping?

The Myth of the Static I.Q.

In our explorations, we have analyzed statistics, evaluated establishments, questioned attitudes of both parents and the professionals, and we have attacked many myths about children. I am an admirer of legends and folklore and certainly enjoy perusing the pages of mythology. When legends are regarded as legends and repeated as legends, they can be both charming and entertaining, but when myths are regarded as truth and are repeated as true, they can be both damaging and undermining.

I have a thorough dislike for "they say" information. "They say" does not make anything so. Someone once wrote that the majority of people have almost always been wrong. In the fourteenth century, the majority thought the world was flat, and that the sun "came up" in the east and "went down" in the west.

One of the dinosaur myths that has hung over little children in particular, and people in general, is that everyone is born with a predetermined mentality level. That is not only a myth, it is a vicious, destructive lie which so limits the potential of individuals that it should be destroyed with dispatch.

And those tests—those godawful so-called intelligence quotient tests that have blighted human potential for years —should be shredded and recycled into toilet paper.

For years, educators and psychologists have insisted that a child's intelligence quotient could not be altered. If he is born dumb, they claimed, he stays dumb. If he is born a genius, he remains a genius. If he is only average, then no matter what, he will stay average.

Those who spewed out such tripe must have had their eyes covered with blinders, and their ears stuffed with cotton. It's a pity that the cotton wasn't stuffed in their mouths and that their pencils were not broken before they had the opportunity to scribble such obscene graffiti on the futures of little children.

Nancy and I long ago learned of the importance placed upon test scores by educators and psychologists who tend to see them as tablets sent down from Mount Sinai. How well we remember the psychologist who guarded a five-year-old Todd's I.Q. scores from our eyes, telling us that such information was "privileged." The privilege of that information was that the psychologist, in godlike tones, predicted that Todd would probably never read beyond the preprimer level and doubtless would never progress beyond the third grade academic level. Obviously, since Todd is now a senior in high school, the psychologist's privileged predictions were wrong.

How frightening it is to think that they might have come true if Nancy and I had respected his opinions as being indisputable and irrevocable—a frightening thought indeed.

Such predictions and such acceptances occur all the time and young children are sorted and cataloged, labeled and limited.

The results of I.Q. tests do not reveal the person's intelligence quotients, potentials, or abilities; they only denote how well the person responded to that particular test. Nothing more. Nothing less.

The greatest lie of all concerning I.Q. scores is that the scores never change or are unlikely to do so; that if a child at five years of age makes a score of 100 (average), he will test out 100 for the rest of his life.

Although parents have questioned the sacrosanctity of these test scores for years, only recently have educators and psychologists joined in open criticism.

In his book *The Modern Family Guide to Education,* Benjamin Fine argues that a person's I.Q. can be raised and stresses that "this is the conviction of leading psychologists and educators who have studied the question of intelligence extensively."[1]

"The Power of Positive Teaching," an article published in *Family Circle,* March 1970, reveals one early study that should have shown the error in regarding an original I.Q. score as a life sentence. The study was conducted in Iowa during the 1930s by psychologist H.A. Skeels. Skeels discovered that the I.Q.s of two mentally retarded children, who had been housed with retarded women for lack of room in an orphanage, had made spectacular gains. Encouraged, he placed a score of other children in wards with retarded adults. All of them improved; the average I.Q. gain being around thirty points, which elevated most of the children into the midnormal range, allowing them to become adoptable. It should be emphasized that these children made their gains not with normal, healthy mothers, but under the care of institutionalized, retarded women.

However, so ingrained was the "professional idea of the immutable I.Q. that Skeels, rather than being treated as a prophet, was dismissed as something of a nut." Giving up psychological research altogether, "vindication came only in the mid-60s when he was able to follow up on nearly all the children in his . . . experiment, and found them leading normal, productive lives, most of them raising normally intelligent children."

In conclusion, the article states: ". . . the concept of the movable I.Q. has been thoroughly established in more than 40 years of research. And if the I.Q. is movable, it must respond to influences."[2]

Pertaining to intelligence tests per se, in his article "Do I.Q. Tests Measure Ability of Your Child?" Arnold Arnold charges:

> There are now many such tests in use other than the standard Stanford-Binet I.Q. Test. But none, to date, measures real and inborn intelligence. . . .
>
> One of the more horrendous effects of reliance on those tests most often used today is that they decide a child's future early in his school career. The school's expectancy and the kind of encouragement given children too often depend on the outcome of tests that are far from reliable.[3]

"I have seen shifts of as much as fifty I.Q. points," declares Dr. Robert Felix, director of the National Institute for Mental Health. "It is not unusual to find increases of from ten to twenty points."[4]

On July 8, 1975, CBS presented a special televised report entitled "The I.Q. Myth." During the course of sixty minutes it was shown how people have been unjustly labeled and limited by the use and abuse of such test scores. Minority and ethnic groups have been carted off to special education classrooms simply because they did not know English well enough to make better grades. Young men have been drafted into the armed services because their scores didn't allow them college deferments. And many immigrants were wrongly classified as dimwitted.

Even though today, when it has been substantiated that I.Q. scores do not reveal a person's intelligence quotient (if there is such a thing), these tests are given to school children en masse and recorded on their permanent records. As the program points out, there is no test which measures motivation and ingenuity. And there is no test to predict whether or not a person will be a success, professionally, or a failure, personally.[5]

If They Get Too Smart, Something Terrible Will Happen!

Another myth which is just as demeaning and destructive in its falsity is that becoming too intelligent makes a person a misfit and stupid in matters of common sense.

We have all been exposed to the absent-minded professor jokes, which in many ways are as degrading as were the little moron jokes of the 1940s and the more recent Polack funnies. Where the Polack stories make fun of and categorize a group of people as mental incompetents who don't know enough to come in out of the rain, the absent-minded professor jokes suggest that too much knowledge clouds a person's awareness of the everyday.

At two o'clock in the morning, the telephone rings at the home of Professor Brightenbach.

The professor answers.

A voice asks, "Is this Plaza 3–4–8–5 thousand?"

"Wait a minute and let me look at the phone," the professor answers. "No, this number is Pl–3–4–8–5–zero–zero–zero."

"I'm sorry to have bothered you," the voice says.

"That's all right," the professor replies, "I had to get up to answer the phone anyway."

See what I mean?

A fast one-liner illustrates the same point more quickly.

"Professor Brightenbach walked into the men's room, unbuttoned his coat, pulled out his tie, and wet his pants."

Apparently, the tellers of such stories and their laughing audiences find some security in rationalizing that there is something wrong with people who are either dumber or smarter than they. It's a strange kind of rationalization.

Psychologists label people who score over 140 points on I.Q. tests as being "gifted." Many strange attitudes have developed about these children and adults. Generally, most people feel that a child, for his own good, should not be encouraged to become too smart.

I recently had a mother tell me, "I don't want my child to get too smart. You know what I mean?"

"No," I answered, "what do you mean?"

"Well, you know," she said, "kids who get too smart are weird. They can't relate to normal people. They hide inside books. I want my child to blend in with normal people—you know, be nice and average."

"Like you and your husband?" I asked.

If looks could kill, I would have been mortally wounded.

"Go to hell!" she quipped and walked away.

The "too smart for their own good" myth is so indelibly written in our minds that we sometimes find it impossible to erase. We have been told that geniuses are eccentric, strange, and weird, and we have believed it.

Nobody Wants a Queer, Genius Kid!

In the article "U.S. Gifted Children Are Neglected," educator Benjamin Fine stresses: "There is an old myth that the gifted child is a child with horn-rimmed glasses, hunchback, and with his face buried in a book. That is not true." Quite the opposite is the case, declares Fine. "They have a large vocabulary. They have an easy way of talking and use words accurately. They are curious, desiring to know the how's and why's of the world around them. They show an early awareness of cause and effect. They want reasons for actions and decisions. Their vocabularies are sprinkled with 'Why?' and 'How come?' and 'Really?'

"For the most part," Fine asserts, "the gifted child is a creative child. He frequently comes up with new solutions to problems and situations. Even at three or four, his vocabulary begins to express itself in creative terms."[6]

C.W. Valentine, author of *The Normal Child,* states that "gifted boys are not effeminate, as is commonly believed. In fact, they slightly exceed other children in their preference for sports, games and hobbies. Most gifted children are avid collectors. Their treasures run from rocks and coins to stamps and books. All gifted children seem to be avid readers. The advanced seven-year-old reads more books in one two-month period than the average child reads throughout the years from 7 to 15. . . ."[7]

C. Etta Walters, Associate Professor of Human Development, Florida State University, affirms:

> . . . Contrary to popular opinion, the gifted child is not queer, sickly, uncoordinated, or unpopular. He is generally above average in physical development and skills; he is well liked by his classmates, and can handle his emotional problems as well, if not better, than his less bright classmates.
>
> The gifted child is superior to children of average intelligence in trustworthiness, in the stability of his moral behavior, and in his emotional, physical and social development.
>
> As an adult, the gifted child is still superior in health and physique. He will have a profession which ranks higher economically and socially than his less intelligent peers.[8]

The "Gifted" Gift

While these good people battle to tear down the myths surrounding "gifted" children, it occurs to me that they are perpetrating still another, and perhaps just as treacherous, myth by calling these children "gifted." Repeatedly, it is suggested that these children have been awarded an unusual intelligence. In reality, perhaps, the only "gift" these children have are exceptional parents or an excellent environment that turned them on at a very early age.

In their article "The Achievers Usually Have Skillful Parents," Thomas J. and Alice Fleming stress:

> What do Henry Ford, John F. Kennedy and Ted Williams have in common?
>
> A burning drive for achievement.
>
> Were they born with it? Most people would say yes, accepting the same fatalistic attitude which has done so much to destroy talent in young people. But today, psychologists know that they are wrong. Achievers are not born, they are created by skillful, knowledgeable parents.[9]

Glenn Doman comments that in reading about childhood geniuses (although they came from a variety of backgrounds and living conditions), time and time again we find that they read before they went to school. "We allowed ourselves to assume that they were able to read at very early ages because they were geniuses. On the other hand, it is just as safe to assume that they became geniuses because they learned to read at a very early age. One thing for sure, no genius in the history of the world taught himself to read—his mother, or his grandmother or his Aunt Sarah had to say, 'Look, kid, this is how it is done.' Someone had to tell him the secret. Just as someone had to tell him the secrets of the spoken word. If we took a potential genius and locked him away in a room somewhere and didn't allow him to hear anyone speak for the first five years of his life, when we brought him out, we certainly wouldn't expect him to say, 'Hi, Mom. Hi, Dad. How have you been?' now would we? Of course not."

If you want to have a "gifted" child it appears that all you have to do is give him the "gift." Start teaching him when he is very young. Answer his questions and watch him grow. Remember, it has been clearly shown that I.Q. scores can be increased as many as fifty points. If you add only forty points to the average 100, you have a "gifted" child.

So why not give him the "gift!"

Chapter 7

How to Create a Creative Child

The Phantom Strikes Again!

Man

A man, out of the depths of what he is, paints a picture, composes a symphony, chisels a sculpture, does an experiment, scales a mountain, promotes a romance, performs a service, accomplishes a kindness. While the means employed may be amenable to understanding, the processes of heart and mind that go into the act of doing are rarely evident even to the doer. He does what he is impelled to do—is at the mercy of his own thoughts and drive. He is the victim of an inner self—a personal demon, as it were —which can be appeased only by release through creativity and achievement.

> —JAY S. HARRISON,
> Music Editor,
> *The New York Tribune*[1]

Ask children what their favorite school subject is, and time after time, the answer will be "art." Yet with all the lip service offered in PTA meetings about individual expression and the nurturing of creative growth, it's surprising, but also a fact, that art is wedged between other subjects in the school curriculum and doled out in miserly segments of time.

Perhaps it's *because* children love drawing and painting so that their explorations with crayon and paint, and their eagerness to attempt any media makes their efforts appear to be play rather than learning. And, unfortunately, most everyone at school seems to believe that learning has to be hard work.

The yearning to create and children's abilities to create do not begin at school, but are evidenced in their very early years. Anyone who has handed a young child a paint brush and jar of paint can surely testify to his enthusiasm to slosh colors on anything within reach. From the time children touch the brush to the time they lay it down, their faces light up and their excited voices twinkle like Christmas bells.

They Are Both the Same—Only Different

Creativity is a fascinating word, as are its associates, create, and creative. According to the *World Book Dictionary,* create is defined as "to cause to be; to bring into being." Creative is "having the power to create, inventive, productive. Approaching the realm of art. Imaginative."

Apparently, almost any visual media—painting, sculpture, drawing, etc.—can be interpreted as being a product of creativity. However, in literature, creative writing is "limited to fiction and poetry." Since I have written fiction, prose, and poetry, as well as factual prose, I would argue into the dark of night that writing factual prose is just as much a creative effort as is writing either fiction or poetry. Perhaps the listing of names and places is rudimentary, but the arrangement of names and places and presenting them in an interesting and lively manner is certainly a creative process into which every self-respecting writer pours his life's blood and emotional energies.

In a recent discussion, an art director insisted that the creation of the visual image was much more difficult and complex than the creation of written composition. He argued at the top of his voice that all the writer has to arrange are words; whereas the artist has to be concerned with color, line, form, texture, point, and space. I calmly yelled back that I thought his argument at best naïve. The words that are available to the writer are as variable as are the visual elements to the artist. I reminded him that I made my living as an illustrator long before I attempted to write a serious piece of prose. I maintain that variables of the creative processes in both visual and written composition are absolutely the same—only they are different. Both writing and illustrating pose to the creator the same pleasures and the same tortures. They both demand that his brain thinks, interprets, and visualizes ahead of his hands.

In his brilliant film *Why Man Creates,* Saul Bass draws the conclusion that people have the desire to create in order to leave their mark for others to see. The reason that some people create graffiti (such as "Kilroy was here") is to remind others that they exist and that their existence is worth being noticed.

There are many who believe that all people are born with the instinct to create. There are some who believe that this inborn urge is the spiritual or God portion of our being. There are others who believe that creativity is a genetic gift of Mankind. There are few who would argue that creativity is not an important and necessary part of Man. However, no matter what people believe, in our culture the creative urges in young children are far too often ignored, and rarely encouraged. Perhaps it is because we tend to see them as being clumsy in their first attempts, or we simply don't believe that they should be taken seriously. Those who do value the abilities and urges of young children find that they are very eager to try anything, and in very short periods of time, can master the skills they are shown.

A Jacquelyn

When I was in the first grade, my teacher looked at a picture I was drawing and said to me, "You're a natural artist." I thought, "Gee, that sounds pretty good," and I hurried home to tell my mother and ask her what the teacher meant. My mother told me that my talent was a gift from

God. I thought it was nice of God to single me out and give me such a gift. To me, the whole thing seemed rather wonderful and spooky.

In retrospect, I'm sure the teacher thought that my drawing ability was a "natural talent." And I'm just as positive that my mother was convinced that it was, indeed, "godgiven." And in listening to other people speak of talents, I am persuaded that the vast majority feel that these are inborn attributes rather than developed ones.

Personally, however, I am convinced that talents are no more inborn than are intelligence quotients. That idea is still another myth we allow to stymie children's potentials. My abilities to draw and paint have nothing to do with inborn qualities, except that I have two hands which can hold pencils and brushes, I have two eyes which can focus on the paper before me, and I have a brain that has the capacity to visualize and organize spacial forms and arrangements.

If the good Lord gave me any special gift, that gift was a cousin who was four years my senior. Jacquelyn was a rather precocious child and most demonstrative about the things she learned. Before I was of school age she let me know, in no uncertain terms, how advanced she was in drawing and painting and reading and writing. And she enjoyed showing me all her accomplishments. She played teacher and I played student. She would hand me crayons and paper and would show me all the tricks she had learned.

"Faces aren't really pink," she would say. "If you color them lightly with orange, they look more like real skin color."

She showed me how to draw trees and houses in perspective. And she made me aware that the sky isn't always blue; sometimes it's orange and pink and purple.

I will never forget that day when Jacquelyn asked in her teacher voice, "What color is the bark on that tree?"

"Black," I answered.

"No," she replied, "look again."

I looked again and answered, "Brown."

"No," she said, "look once more."

I looked and looked, until I thought my eyes were going to fall out of my head.

"I don't know," I finally said, hating to admit defeat.

"Come here and I'll show you," she said. I followed her to the tree.

"Now, look closely," she instructed. When I did, I saw what she meant. The bark on the tree was a combination of many colors. There were purples and blues and reds and greens and yellows and greys. She was right. The bark on the tree wasn't just black or bown.

At any rate, when I entered Miss Oldham's first grade class, I could draw and paint as well as most fourth graders. But what she had mistaken for a natural talent wasn't a talent at all—it was a Jacquelyn.

Very few people really seem to understand this. They often say they do but they don't. I often tell this story and people nod their heads at the conclusion. Then I ask, "Do you know what that means? It means that every child can become an artist or a writer or an architect or a designer or whatever, if someone takes the time to teach him at a very early age."

Then the people who just finished saying they understood, wrinkle their foreheads and ask, "Do you really believe that?"

People who create realize that this is true. About four years ago I did a series of layouts for a book that Glenn Doman was writing. They were extremely difficult to do and I had spent a month of twenty-four days to complete them in time for him to present them to the publisher. As he was looking at them for the first time, his office was crowded with other people peering over our shoulders. These weren't people off the street and out of the hallways. They were doctors, educators, therapists, etc.

When we were finished, one of the educators (the very one who should have known better), said, "Gee, it must be nice to have talent."

Without looking up, Glenn replied, "These layouts have

nothing to do with talent. They are the result of preparation, discipline and a hell of a lot of hard work."

Liza Minnelli once told me that if one more person told her how lucky she was to have her mother's talents, she thought she would scream. "They think everything I do was given to me," Liza said. "Let me tell you something. I certainly learned a lot from my mother and my father, but nothing was given to me. I've had to work hard to be able to do the things I do. People seem to ignore the summer stock plays I was in, and the years I traveled doing one-night stands. It's not called talent; it's called discipline."

I once asked Liza why, after witnessing all the trials and tribulations her mother endured, she decided to become a performer. She responded, "I didn't think I was pretty enough to be a secretary."

Repeatedly, we read and hear "talented" people declare that the difference between the mediocre and the superb is discipline and concentration. Katharine Hepburn says that Spencer Tracy was a superb actor because he had the power of total concentration. Singers speak of concentration. Writers know its importance. I have never heard an actor or a performer or an athlete say that he excelled because he was talented. He doesn't say it because he knows better. He realizes that through hard work and a great deal of discipline and concentration, it appears that he is talented.

It is extremely important for parents to realize that children have the ability not only to learn multiplication tables, but that they can become architects. It is important for parents to realize that children can not only learn about language, but that they can utilize and mold that language into forceful prose and sensitive poetry. It is important for parents to become aware that it is their duty not only to recognize talent when it hits them in the face, but it is their duty to nurture the creativity in children so that talents can develop.

Down with the Talent Myth

The misuse of the word *talent* has really screwed up the ways people look at creativity. It seems many have convinced themselves that people create because they have talent. It is the exact opposite. People have talent because they create. It is after they create that others recognize their talent, not vice versa. Who would have known that Joan Sutherland was a talented singer if she had not worked to create that discipline called an operatic voice? If Dali had not created those marvelous plastic, liquid, and weightless shapes, who would have known the man possessed artistic talent? And if Truman Capote had not served *Breakfast at Tiffany's* or reminded us of *A Christmas Memory,* or if he had not chilled us *In Cold Blood,* how should we have known that he is a "talented" writer?

Perhaps the ultimate in the creative process is that "magic time" when the artist, whether he's a painter, writer, singer, engineer, architect, actor, or whatever, is able to draw the thought processes from the brain and converge those thoughts into direct lines.

"Creativity is a child's most valuable asset," writes Jean E. Laird, in her article "Creativity: Your Greatest Gift to Your Child," "because he has not yet learned all the popular views and answers. And his creativity is vital to our society. 'Parents and teachers may either foster or suppress creative tendencies in children,' " she quotes Dr. Arnold Gesell, of the Gesell Institute of Child Development. " 'Indifference is a deterrent. If no one cares about his wonderful new ideas, the child may no longer bother to express them.' "

The article continued to relate that a study at the University of Chicago, conducted by two psychologists, Jacob W. Getzels and Phillip W. Jackson, found certain factors characteristic of families with highly creative children. ". . . The family interests were broad and varied, thus stimulating the children's inborn curiosity. The atmosphere was generally relaxed; and the parents were able to meet most normal stresses without undue tension or worry, recovering very well when more serious strains were present. They also found time for nonsense and good-natured humor."[2]

It is frequently noticed that so-called talented and so-called creative people tend to be so-called multitalented. Painters become writers and actors become painters and so on. There is nothing strange about that. These people have learned to excel in one certain area—they have learned to express themselves. They have learned the trick of being creative and the trick of being talented. Once a person conquers one media they aren't afraid to attempt another. Actors are a good example. Jane Wyman is a terrific artist, so are Hedy Lamarr, Lili Palmer, Kim Novak, Red Skelton, and Jonathan Winters. And so were Lionel Barrymore, Richard Whorf, and Edward G. Robinson. Practically all singers have the ability to become good actors. And why not? Isn't singing a song a form of dramatic expression?

Consequently, if you teach your child to be "talented" or "creative" in one media, chances are, he will eventually become "talented" or "creative" in a number of fields of endeavor.

Creative people also become highly individualistic.

Getzels and Jackson recently made a study to analyze the difference between intelligence and creativity. They used two groups of students. One group consisted of students who scored in the upper 20 percent on I.Q. tests, with the other group scoring high on tests for creativity. There was an average of twenty-three points difference between the high I.Q. group and the creative group.

Getzels and Jackson found that the "noncreative high I.Q.'s tended to be model students, precise, regular, obedient, and favorites of their teachers. The creative types, on the other hand, were often troublesome to the teachers. They expressed themselves with ". . . irreverence, unexpected . . . metaphors, sidewise leaps and in fact general freedom of bounds."[3]

It might be concluded from the Getzels-Jackson study that

creative people are more difficult to handle. Or it may be an indication that constant regimentation tends to frustrate them and, as a result, they rebel. One thing is certain. If we want to maintain and nurture the individual in this country, there is no better insurance than producing creative people. They do not make willing or obedient slaves. They think for themselves.

It also appears that those children who are encouraged and given the opportunities to be creative from a very early age become imaginative adults. And those who aren't, don't. Or at least their chances are greatly lessened.

"Creativity was in each of us as a small child," Harold H. Anderson, research professor of Michigan State University is quoted as saying. "Among adults it is almost nonexistent. The question is, what has happened to this enormous and universal human resource?" The answer, Anderson believes, is that our colossal system of education "is concerned mainly with acquiring a body of knowledge, memorizing of facts, and finding answers to problems, all of which are already known to someone else, rather than with creativity."[4]

A Theory Worth the Ponder

It is now concluded that each of us has within the confines of his skull, two brains instead of one—a left brain and a right brain. The left brain is responsible for the functions of the right side of our bodies, and the right brain is responsible for the functions of the left side of our bodies. It has been established that one brain controls speech patterns and the other brain controls rhythm or musical patterns. The speech pattern side is often referred to as the dominant side and is in about 85 percent of us the left brain. Therefore, about 85 percent of us are right-handed. The other brain is usually referred to as the subdominant side.

Carl Delacato, Ed.D., has written and lectured much on the subject of the committed cortex and the importance of the establishment of complete dominance in one side of the brain. Dr. Delacato has an interesting theory which he sensibly labels as a "theory." He suspects that there is a strong possibility that the two brains are incorrectly labeled as dominant and subdominant. Instead, they should be labeled as "academic" and "creative," the speech side being responsible for academic thought patterns, and the musical side responsible for creative patterns.

In many ways, Delacato's theory of the "academic" and the "creative" brains makes good sense. In the last few years, I have had the opportunity to talk with a number of writers. The one question I am always led to ask is, "How do you write?" Uniformly, they answer that they go through rituals to prepare themselves to begin. Some writers require an hour of preparation before finally writing a word. This seems to be true also of artists. It is a legitimate question to ask if this time of preparation is only to sharpen pencils and stack paper or if it is used to get an idea. Or, is this the time required by them to switch their thought processes from the "academic" brain to the "creative" brain? It's an interesting question.

I hear so much about creative moods. Many writers and illustrators maintain that the "creative mood" is, in reality, the ability to function on another level of thought patterns. Some even feel that they may mentally transcend into a hypnotic state before they can create. I think there is a certain validity in those observations because I have personally found that creative processes often seem to come from another plane of awareness.

I have a unique quirk in my work—I can never remember anything I have written. My friend Rod McKuen has the same quirk. Although he can easily sing his own songs, even in concert, he has to read his poetry rather than trust his memory.

What does this mean? Does it mean that Rod and I have short memories? I don't think so. I can recite "I must go down to the sea again" and any number of stanzas written by other people, and I know Rod can too. Perhaps it means, then, that our left brains don't always know what our right brains are doing. And perhaps it means that people are, indeed, schizophrenic—two people housed in one head—a creative person and an academic person.

A quick experiment will show you how this works. Stop reading for a moment and try to recite the lyrics of a song without humming the tune. You'll find it is quite difficult to do because you have learned the song in your "tonality" or "creative" brain, and without the tune you are asking your "speech" or "academic" brain to recite the lines. Since your "academic" brain has also heard the lines, it will respond with some of the stanzas, but start humming the tune and the words will start flowing from your "creative" brain without effort.

Doctors often observe the same phenomenon in stroke patients. Those persons who have strokes in their "speech" brain have difficulty in talking, but have no difficulty in singing. Those who have suffered an injury to their "tonality" brain, may have no difficulty in speaking, but are tone deaf.

Now, what does this have to do with children? The indications are that in teaching children, we are presenting information to not only one brain, but two. Possibly during their early years and during their schooling, we concentrate on the academic person and ignore the creative one. We feed the "academic" brain but we starve the "creative" one. I would not propose that we switch our emphasis and feed mainly the "creative" brain and starve the "academic" one, but I don't feel that the suggestion of feeding both with information and learning experiences would be out of order.

I am not saying that all people must create if they are to be whole and complete, but it would be nice if it were their own choice. And there is strong evidence that most children do not have that choice because their creative development has been limited. Nor am I proposing that creativity will insure happiness any more than I would propose that academic scholarship will insure financial success. But I am proposing that we give young children every opportunity to develop to their fullest potentials, thus broadening the spectrum of their abilities.

My wish is that everyone would begin looking at children, not as little people, but as little geniuses ready to explore and learn. I wish we could throw away the godgiven talent myth and realize that all children can have talent if they are allowed to create. Someone once said, "Inside every fat person there is a thin person trying to get out." I wish that everyone would realize that inside every little child there is a talented genius trying to get out.

Future Picassos, Dalis, and Disneys

Would you like to teach your preschooler to be an artist? You can if you like. It's easy.

You begin by showing him reproductions of the world's great masterpieces and as you're looking at the pictures, talk about the paintings and how they were painted. For instance, say, "Oh, look at what the artist has done here. Hasn't he used light in a beautiful way?" And, "Aren't these sunflowers lovely! Look, you can see the brush marks. See how thick the paint is." And, "Hasn't the artist given a wonderful feeling of movement in this pencil sketch?" And so on.

Now, someone may say, "That sounds like a college art appreciation course. Isn't that too difficult for a little kid to understand?" What is difficult about pencil marks or thickness of paint? When one compares those things with the task of learning a complete hearing, speaking, writing language, they are simple, indeed. What you are doing is enhancing your child's awareness of visual communications.

Don't expect your child to immediately respond to everything you tell him. Don't be test happy. It's not a "let's review the pages we covered this morning" situation. If you test your child too often, the kid says to himself, "Here we go again. Either she doesn't remember what she told me or she's trying to find out if I was listening."

Children catch on to that game all too quickly. Testing is repetitious and takes the fun out of the whole thing. You see, in teaching your child a language, if you taught him only one word at a time and waited until he repeated that one word before you began to teach him a new one, by the time he was ninety-one years old he might be able to say a simple sentence.

In teaching the young child, you are programming the most magnificent computer ever designed. If the computer programmer required the computer to respond to each piece of information he placed into the machine before he added another piece of information, it would take years and years to fill the machine's memory banks. And by the time they were filled, much of the information would be outdated and outmoded.

You don't have to test your child. If you keep placing good and correct information into him, he will start responding to it without your urging him to do so. And better still, he will apply that information to new encounters. Some morning he will bring a book or a magazine to you and say, "Look what the artist has done in this painting. The colors are really beautiful." Or he might say, "I'd like this color on my wall." When he begins to do this, he is doing better than answering the questions to some test you might design; he is applying the information you have given him in meaningful ways. And don't think that it is going to take him years and years to do this. It will happen very quickly and naturally.

If you would like to teach your child to draw and paint, you can begin to teach him as soon as you think he is ready. That's probably not true—you can begin as soon as you think *you* are ready. Actually, he is probably ready to learn long before you feel confident enough to teach him.

Buy some crayons and large sheets of paper. Remember Suzuki's method. Don't say, "Come here, kid, I'm going to teach you to draw. Now sit down, shut your mouth and watch and listen." *You* sit down with *your* crayons and *your* paper and begin drawing or painting. Anything that interests you will interest your child. You might hum a little. When an adult starts humming, no kid can resist wondering what the big one is up to now. He'll soon start nudging his way in between you and the table.

Don't be too eager to hand him the crayons or the brush. Let both his curiosity and his eagerness mount. Let him first get the idea that you enjoy drawing and painting, and that they are accepted adult things to do. Finally, when you hand him a crayon and a piece of paper, let him know that you are doing him a favor.

Your sense of timing is extremely important. Always stop and put the materials away just before he becomes tired of the project. Not too soon, before he feels a sense of accomplishment, but don't wait until he sees something he would rather do. It's like ice cream—give him enough of it to enjoy, but not enough to make him sick.

Be sure that the paper is large—at least eighteen by twenty-four inches—and encourage your youngster to work in large, sweeping motions. Don't be tempted to buy the ready-made coloring books. They only limit your child's creativity.

And don't start showing him how he can draw a circle and by adding two elongated shapes for ears, he can make a rabbit. A rabbit indeed! He'll have a circle and two elongated shapes and only to amuse you and comfort your whim, will he agree that it does sort of look like a rabbit.

Many advisors believe that a blackboard and chalk are excellent creative tools for the child. That shows how little respect they have for the child's creative products. The quick eraser only teaches the child that nothing lasts forever and sometimes not even for two minutes. I remember when I was in first grade I hated to make drawings on the blackboard because I knew that no matter how good they were or how much I liked the pictures, they would soon be obliterated to make room for someone else's work. Let your child learn that the work he does has a permanency to it.

Don't encourage him to try to draw small detail with crayons. Crayons are miserable things to use in small work.

The points don't stay sharpened beyond one or two strokes. They are really the crudest of art tools.

I recently designed a layout for a book jacket. Since the book, entitled *Happy Birthday, America!,* features artwork of gradeschool children, I decided the lettering should be done with crayons. I made a quick trip to the nearest dime store, bought what was once a ten-cent box of crayons for fifty cents, and hurried home to complete the layout. I figured that in about ten minutes the lettering would be finished. The point broke on the first letter and little bits of oily color shattered and scattered all over my nice clean cover. Three hours later I was still laboring with the thing and the language spewing from my studio was unfit for human ears. I don't see how children use the damned things!

The same is true for the big, wide brushes found in most kindergartens—they are almost impossible to manage. If you are uncomfortable using any materials then don't give them to your child, because he is bound to find them uncomfortable too. It is really a tribute to their persistence and their eagerness to create that children overcome such formidable obstacles.

The best way for you to teach your child to paint is to get an easel for yourself and simply start painting. Do you have to run out and first take a quickie art course? Good heavens no! Get some water colors and some paper and start experimenting with the colors. Most of you already know how to paint, and it certainly doesn't take very long to get back into the swing of it. Your child learns from your enjoyment.

We used to be told in school that it was very difficult to become an artist; that one has to work and work and study and study. That's complete and utter gobbledygook. What those teachers meant was that *they* would have to work and work and study and study for years and years before they could do anything worthwhile. But that's not true of kids. All you have to do is have the materials and show them how to use them, and away they go. I recently saw a set of slides taken at the TEM (Talent Education Movement) School in

Japan. Two-year-olds and three-year-olds were painting, beautiful pictures—not circular faces and triangular ears, but gorgeous water colors. These were not exceptional kids who had been selected from the mainstream. They were simply kids who had been given the opportunity to paint.

And get some modeling clay. Not only do kids love to mold it, but it's a great means by which their manual dexterity can be improved. Don't buy just one little chunk, so that like chalk drawings on a blackboard, the child's products must be destroyed to replace other creative efforts. Don't try to teach production and destruction at the same time.

Most of all—have fun! And be sure your child has fun. "Ooh" and "Aah" over his latest work and be sure to display his efforts.

The most difficult part of teaching is to retain the spontaniety so that the time spent with your child does not become regimented. It is not twice as good to catch him at the peak of his interest—it is a thousand times better. The time you spend with him should be a treat, never a threat.

Future Casals, Heifetzes and Brubecks

If you want your child to become a musician, start programming him at a very early age. Don't rely on the radio for music selections. Borrow albums from the library and buy some of your own. Play all kinds of music—classical, jazz, popular, etc.—from the time you first bring your baby home from the hospital. And start talking to him about the sounds he hears. Check to see if your community has a Suzuki school nearby.

If either parent plays an instrument, play it often.

If you want your child to be creative or talented, you as parents can give him the "gift." Talent is not a genetic endowment. It is presented to children by loving and sensitive parents in a warm and caring home.

Chapter 8

How to Compare Your Child's Development

Breaking the Rules

The two greatest events in every human life and the two most commonly celebrated with recognized satisfaction by all are those of (1) birth, and (2) attainment of the free, unaided, upright state of locomotion called walking.

. . . Walking is not just putting one foot before the other in an upright position to move from here to there. It is the highest symphony of movement, coordination, balance and timing so far perfected for moving a heavy mass from place to place with ease and satisfaction.

—TEMPLE FAY, M.D.[1]

Repeatedly, I hear mothers say, "I wish I had some way to evaluate my child's development so I would know where he is in relationship to other children his age."

Repeatedly, the professionals have answered, "Naughty, naughty. That's bad because it turns mothers into anxious ogres who *pressure, pressure, pressure* their little children!"

The professionals insisted that it is better to wait until the children enter school where they can be tested, sorted into categories, and where the professionals can *pressure, pressure, pressure* them into nice, neat packages.

However, the brighter professionals are beginning to catch on to what many parents have known for years. Comparing children's abilities during preschool years does not mean we have to label or restrict them. Instead, we can use the comparisons as guidelines to enhance their growth patterns.

In the article "Early Learning," Sister Margaret Erhart, R.S.C.J., of the Maryville Early Learning Center, St. Louis, Missouri, is quoted saying: "What we eventually would like to know is how a child's mind is working at a certain age. If we know where a child is along the developmental scale at these early ages we can cue in and help him along."[2]

If these first five years of a child's life are so important, and certainly we have seen enough evidence to prove that they are, then isn't it obvious that an evaluation at age five is not soon enough?

If mothers are going to be able to alter the learning capacities of their children at a time when they are most alterable, isn't it clear that mothers need a birth evaluation tool; a six-month evaluation tool; a two-year evaluation tool? In fact, they need an evaluation tool which they can use any time they choose, and one with certain prerequisites:

•The important developmental stages would be defined.
•It would be easy to understand.
•It would be easy to use.
•It should have adjustable time frames.

Glenn Doman realized that proper goals must be established for brain-injured children. Of course, among the staff and mothers there were many goals devised for each of these children. They were good goals. For instance, a mother who had a blind child wanted her child to see. A mother of a paralyzed child wanted her child to move. And the mother of a functionally deaf child wanted her child to hear.

The goals seemed to be clear-cut and well-defined. Often, as the children's conditions improved, the goals were altered and redefined.

"A mother would tell me," Doman says, " 'If my child could just crawl across the floor, I'd be happy.'

"At the time, these mothers meant what they said. But months later, when a child was able to crawl across the floor, her qualifications for happiness changed. She'd say, 'Yes, that's pretty good, but when is he going to walk?' These mothers drove us crazy with their slide-rule prerequisites for happiness. Then, finally, we would have a real confrontation. The mother would enter my office showing that she was rather annoyed. When I'd ask what the problem was she would say, 'Johnny's been walking for six months, but he still hasn't won one footrace!'

"I would go home at night and think, 'Good God, what's the matter with that mother? After one of those experiences, I said to myself, 'That woman is not going to be pleased even if that kid can do everything that every other kid can do. She's not going to be happy until he's better than other kids.' Then I stopped cold and realized that that was exactly right. And wasn't that kid lucky to have such a mother.

"So," Doman says, "we realized that the goal we had to establish for each brain-injured child would have to be 'normality' because mothers weren't going to be happy with anything less. Nor should they be."

As Doman explains, he thought it would be a simple task for him to find what was considered to be the normal development of a child—a five-minute trip to the library, walk in, go to the bookshelves, and take down a book called *The Normal Development of Children.* He soon found there was no such book. Only occasionally in the midst of all the trivia did he find mentioned the really important levels of child development—reference to the child's "preference of handedness" or at what age a child takes his first steps. He found the same to be true in "doctor's advice-to-mothers books"—long sections on potty training and drooling and diaper rash, but so little information was offered which simply stated, "These are the things you should expect your child to do and these are the ages at which he should do them."

Glenn Doman decided that if there were going to be a proper tool with which the neurological development of children could be compared with the "normal" or "average," then he was going to have to design such a tool. And that is exactly what he did.

At this point one might ask, "What does Melton think he's

doing? Isn't he the guy who supposedly doesn't like tests and isn't he about to give mothers just that to use with their kids?" Yes, this is the guy who is cautious of tests, and, no, I'm not giving mothers a test that labels or limits either their views or their child's abilities or potentials.

The Doman-Delacato Developmental Profile is not a test. It's an evaluation tool; a comparative tool. It does not have a pass or fail system. It helps a mother learn at what levels her child is functioning at the present time, and tells her what the next step in his development should be.

In the following pages I will present The Doman-Delacato Developmental Profile at length, because it is more than an important piece of paper. It is the story of children's lives— all children's. It tells clearly how children develop from birth to the neurological age of seventy-two months.

There will be many a mother who will quickly turn the pages to find the areas where she can compare her child's development. Then she may read to find what will be the next level of development she can expect or encourage. I consider that cheating. However, I am not opposed to mothers cheating to improve the lot of their children.

I am not going to tell you that you must read every word or your child's life may be in danger, but I am going to suggest that if first you read all the stages of The Profile before comparing your child's development, you may have a better and more complete picture of these fascinating creatures we call infants, babies, and children.

But first let me warn you of two things:

1) Don't be surprised if there are few or no surprises. I have noticed that when The Profile is presented to mothers, they tend to say, "Of course, that's true—that's exactly how children grow." Since The Profile reflects the "average" or "normal" development of children, that is precisely what their reactions should be.

2) The Doman-Delacato Developmental Profile is a statement of how things are under the present conditions which have been generally accepted in the rearing of children. How-

ever, it is not a prediction that those are the conditions which must remain. As most mothers will quickly realize, The Profile, like brain growth, is not a static and irrevocable pattern, but it is an adjustable slide rule.

Thousands of mothers throughout the world have already adjusted that slide rule by teaching their babies to read and accelerating the development of their children. As we have seen in this book, several studies have found that when infants are placed in a poor neurological environment, they progress at slower rates. As you explore these levels of children's development, the most important thing for you to remember is that there is a good deal of scientific and empirical evidence that the abilities and the neurological organization of children are a direct reflection of the environment we have created around their early years. Many of these conditions can be altered. Children can be brighter and more active if we make their environments more conducive to producing brighter and more active children.

"The Doman-Delacato Developmental Profile serves as a model of human development in a number of ways," says Gretchen Kerr, Director of the Children's Institutes of The Institutes for the Achievement of Human Potential:

> First, it is divided into the *sensory* side of vision (seeing), auditory sense (hearing), and tactile sense (feeling), which are the pathways through which information about the environment goes into the brain, and the *motor* side of mobility, language and manual competence (hand function) which are the pathways through which the brain can respond to the environment.
>
> Second, The Profile serves as a model of the sequence in which the brain matures and the time in which this occurs.
>
> Third, it is a model of the sequence of development of specific functions that a human being must accomplish to achieve complete neurological development.[3]

THE DOMAN-DELACATO DEVELOPMENTAL PROFILE BY GLENN J DOMAN, CARL H DELACATO ED D, ROBERT J DOMAN M D	MOBILITY	LANGUAGE	MANUAL COMPETENCE
	Using a leg in a skilled role which is consistent with the dominant hemisphere	Complete vocabulary and proper sentence structure	Using a hand to write which is consistent with the dominant hemisphere
	Walking and running in complete cross pattern	2000 words of language and short sentences	Bimanual function with one hand in a dominant role
	Walking with arms freed from the primary balance role	10 to 25 words of language and two word couplets	Cortical opposition bilaterally and simultaneously
	Walking with arms used in a primary balance role most frequently at or above shoulder height	Two words of speech used spontaneously and meaningfully	Cortical opposition in either hand
	Creeping on hands and knees, culminating in cross pattern creeping	Creation of meaningful sounds	Prehensile grasp
	Crawling in the prone position culminating in cross pattern crawling	Vital crying in response to threats to life	Vital release
THE INSTITUTES FOR THE ACHIEVEMENT OF HUMAN POTENTIAL 8801 STENTON AVENUE PHILADELPHIA, PA. 19118	Movement of arms and legs without bodily movement	Birth cry and crying	Grasp reflex

BRAIN STAGE		TIME FRAME	VISUAL COMPETENCE	AUDITORY COMPETENCE	TACTILE COMPETENCE
VII	SOPHISTI-CATED CORTEX	Superior 36 Mon. Average 72 Mon. Slow 108 Mon.	Reading words using a dominant eye consistent with the dominant hemisphere	Understanding of 2000 words and simple sentences	Tactile identification of objects using a hand consistent with hemispheric dominance
VI	PRIMITIVE CORTEX	Superior 22 Mon. Average 36 Mon. Slow 70 Mon.	Identification of visual symbols and letters within experience	Understanding of complete vocabulary and proper sentences with proper ear	Description of objects by tactile means
V	EARLY CORTEX	Superior 13 Mon. Average 18 Mon. Slow 36 Mon.	Differentiation of similar but unlike simple visual symbols	Understanding of 10 to 25 words and two word couplets	Tactile differentiation of similar but unlike objects
IV	INITIAL CORTEX	Superior 8 Mon. Average 12 Mon. Slow 22 Mon.	Convergence of vision resulting in simple depth perception	Understanding of two words of speech	Tactile understanding of the third dimension in objects which appear to be flat
III	MIDBRAIN	Superior 4 Mon. Average 7 Mon. Slow 12 Mon.	Appreciation of detail within a configuration	Appreciation of meaningful sounds	Appreciation of gnostic sensation
II	PONS	Superior 1 Mon. Average 2.5 Mon. Slow 4 Mon.	Outline perception	Vital response to threatening sounds	Perception of vital sensation
I	MEDULLA and CORD	Superior Birth to .5 Average Birth to 1.0 Slow Birth to 1.5	Light reflex	Startle reflex	Babinski reflex

BRAIN STAGE		TIME FRAME	VISUAL COMPETENCE
VII	SOPHISTI-CATED CORTEX	Superior 36 Mon. Average 72 Mon. Slow 108 Mon.	**Reading words using a dominant eye consistent with the dominant hemisphere**
VI	PRIMITIVE CORTEX	Superior 22 Mon. Average 36 Mon. Slow 70 Mon.	**Identification of visual symbols and letters within experience**
V	EARLY CORTEX	Superior 13 Mon. Average 18 Mon. Slow 36 Mon.	**Differentiation of similar but unlike simple visual symbols**
IV	INITIAL CORTEX	Superior 8 Mon. Average 12 Mon. Slow 22 Mon.	**Convergence of vision resulting in simple depth perception**
III	MIDBRAIN	Superior 4 Mon. Average 7 Mon. Slow 12 Mon.	**Appreciation of detail within a configuration**
II	PONS	Superior 1 Mon. Average 2.5 Mon. Slow 4 Mon.	**Outline perception**
I	MEDULLA and CORD	Superior Birth to .5 Average Birth to 1.0 Slow Birth to 1.5	**Light reflex**

Visual Competence

The First Developmental Level of a child's visual competence is *light reflex.* At birth, babies are functionally blind, but their eyes respond immediately to a bright light by the pupils' dilating reflexively. When the light is taken away, the pupils dilate. This will occur as often as the light is presented and removed.

The Second Developmental Level of a child's visual competence is *outline perception.* At this stage the baby begins to see silhouettes of people and objects.

If a baby has outline perception at 2.5 months, his development of visual competence is rated *average.*

If a baby has outline perception at 1 month, his development of visual competence is rated *superior.*

If a baby does *not* have outline perception until 4 months, his development of visual competence is rated *slow.*

The Third Developmental Level of a child's visual competence is appreciation of *detail within a configuration.* Now the baby begins to see the mother's face rather than just a shadowy outline and can see a painted design on a plastic cup instead of just the gross outline of the object.

If a baby has an appreciation of detail within a configuration at 7 months, his development of visual competence is rated *average.*

If a baby has an appreciation of detail within a configuration at 4 months, his development of visual competence is rated *superior.*

If a baby does *not* have an appreciation of detail within a configuration until he is 12 months, his development of visual competence is rated *slow.*

The Fourth Developmental Level of a child's visual competence is *convergence of vision resulting in simple depth perception.* Now the child can coordinate his eyes to focus on an object and blend the images received by both eyes, and he can realize that objects have depth as well as height and width.

> If a child has convergence of vision resulting in simple depth perception at 12 months, his development of visual competence is rated *average.*
>
> If a child has convergence of vision resulting in simple depth perception at 8 months, his development of visual competence is rated *superior.*
>
> If a child does *not* have convergence of vision resulting in simple depth perception until 22 months, his development of visual competence is rated *slow.*

The Fifth Developmental Level of a child's visual competence is *differentiation of similar but unlike simple visual symbols.* Although on a printed page a red ball and a red apple may appear to be similar, the child can now recognize the difference between the two.

> If a child can differentiate between similar but unlike simple visual symbols at 18 months, his development of visual competence is rated *average.*
>
> If a child can differentiate between similar but unlike simple visual symbols at 13 months, his development of visual competence is rated *superior.*
>
> If a child *cannot* differentiate between similar but unlike simple visual symbols until 36 months, his development of visual competence is rated *slow.*

The Sixth Developmental Level of a child's visual competence is *identification of visual symbols and letters within experience.* Now a child can recognize some of the letters of the alphabet, triangles, circles, or even printed words (if, of course, he has had the opportunity of someone's telling him what they are or has been able to draw conclusions from experience).

If a child can identify visual symbols and letters within his experience at 36 months, his development of visual competence is rated *average*.

If a child can identify visual symbols and letters within his experience at 22 months, his development of visual competence is rated *superior*.

If a child *cannot* identify visual symbols and letters within his experience until 70 months, his development of visual competence is rated *slow*.

The Seventh Developmental Level of a child's visual competence is *reading words using a dominant eye consistent with the dominant hemisphere*. One eye is a leader; one eye is a follower. If a child is using his right eye as the leader, the chances are good that his left brain hemisphere is dominant. If his neurological development is proper, he is right-eyed, right-eared, right-handed, and right-footed. Or he may be consistently left-sided; it makes little difference so long as one side is consistently dominant.

If a child can read words using a dominant eye consistent with the dominant hemisphere at 72 months, his development of visual competence is rated *average*.

If a child can read words using a dominant eye consistent with the dominant hemisphere at 36 months, his development of visual competence is rated *superior*.

If a child *cannot* read words using a dominant eye consistent with the dominant hemisphere until 108 months, his development of visual competence is rated *slow*.

	BRAIN STAGE	TIME FRAME	AUDITORY COMPETENCE
VII	SOPHISTI-CATED CORTEX	Superior 36 Mon. Average 72 Mon. Slow 108 Mon.	**Understanding of complete vocabulary and proper sentences with proper ear**
VI	PRIMITIVE CORTEX	Superior 22 Mon. Average 36 Mon. Slow 70 Mon.	**Understanding of 2000 words and simple sentences**
V	EARLY CORTEX	Superior 13 Mon. Average 18 Mon. Slow 36 Mon.	**Understanding of 10 to 25 words and two word couplets**
IV	INITIAL CORTEX	Superior 8 Mon. Average 12 Mon. Slow 22 Mon.	**Understanding of two words of speech**
III	MIDBRAIN	Superior 4 Mon. Average 7 Mon. Slow 12 Mon.	**Appreciation of meaningful sounds**
II	PONS	Superior 1 Mon. Average 2.5 Mon. Slow 4 Mon.	**Vital response to threatening sounds**
I	MEDULLA and CORD	Superior Birth to .5 Average Birth to 1.0 Slow Birth to 1.5	**Startle reflex**

Auditory Competence

The First Developmental Level of a child's auditory competence is *startle reflex,* which is present at birth. If there is a loud, sharp noise close by, the baby will react with a jerk, and he will react in the same manner as often as the noise is made.

The Second Developmental Level of a child's auditory competence is *vital response to threatening sounds.* Now, when the baby hears harsh, loud noises, he will cry, thus sounding his alarm system to alert his mother.

If a child has a vital response to threatening sounds at 2.5 months, his development of auditory competence is rated *average.*

If a child has a vital response to threatening sounds at 1 month, his development of auditory competence is rated *superior.*

If a child does *not* have a vital response to threatening sounds until 4 months, his development of auditory competence is rated *slow.*

The Third Developmental Level of a child's auditory competence is *appreciation of meaningful sounds.* Now the baby begins to respond to the mother's voice and to pleasant sounds as well as harsh noises. He begins to realize which is which.

If a baby has appreciation of meaningful sounds at 7 months, his development of auditory competence is rated *average.*

If a baby has appreciation of meaningful sounds at 4 months, his development of auditory competence is rated *superior.*

If a baby does *not* have appreciation of meaningful

sounds until 12 months, his development of auditory competence is rated *slow*.

The Fourth Developmental Level of a child's auditory competence is *understanding of two words of speech*. What is the best way for a mother to test when a baby understands two words of speech? If a mother thinks her baby understands two words, you can believe her. She knows.

If a child has an understanding of two words of speech at 12 months, his development of auditory competence is rated *average*.

If a child has an understanding of two words of speech at 8 months, his development of auditory competence is rated *superior*.

If a child does *not* have an understanding of two words of speech until 22 months, his development of auditory competence is rated *slow*.

The Fifth Developmental Level of a child's auditory competence is *an understanding of 10 to 25 words and 2-word couplets* (big ball, come here, etc.).

If a child has an understanding of 10 to 25 words and 2-word couplets at 18 months, his development of auditory competence is rated *average*.

If a child has an understanding of 10 to 25 words and 2-word couplets at 13 months, his development of auditory competence is rated *superior*.

If a child does *not* have an understanding of 10 to 25 words and 2-word couplets until 36 months, his development of auditory competence is rated *slow*.

The Sixth Developmental Level of a child's auditory competence is *an understanding of 2,000 words and simple sentences*. Once you realize that your child understands more words than you care to count, you know that chances are he has reached the 2,000 mark, and of course you realize whether he understands simple sentences.

If a child has an understanding of 2,000 words and simple sentences at 36 months, his development of auditory competence is rated *average*.

If a child has an understanding of 2,000 words and simple sentences at 22 months, his development of auditory competence is rated *superior*.

If a child does *not* have an understanding of 2,000 words and simple sentences until 70 months, his development of auditory competence is rated *slow*.

The Seventh Developmental Level of a child's auditory competence is *an understanding of complete vocabulary and proper sentences with proper ear*. Now you have to close the door if you want to say anything you do not want him to repeat or tell the neighbors. If he is consistently right-eyed, right-handed, right-footed, he should also be right-eared. If he tries to listen to soft sounds, such as a watch ticking, he will consistently place the object to his right ear.

If a child has an understanding of complete vocabulary and proper sentences with proper ear at 72 months, his development of auditory competence is rated *average*.

If a child has an understanding of complete vocabulary and proper sentences with proper ear at 36 months, his development of auditory competence is rated *superior*.

If a child does *not* have an understanding of complete vocabulary and proper sentences with proper ear until 108 months, his development of auditory competence is rated *slow*.

BRAIN STAGE		TIME FRAME	TACTILE COMPETENCE
VII	SOPHISTI-CATED CORTEX	Superior 36 Mon. Average 72 Mon. Slow 108 Mon.	Tactile identification of objects using a hand consistent with hemispheric dominance
VI	PRIMITIVE CORTEX	Superior 22 Mon. Average 36 Mon. Slow 70 Mon.	Description of objects by tactile means
V	EARLY CORTEX	Superior 13 Mon. Average 18 Mon. Slow 36 Mon.	Tactile differentiation of similar but unlike objects
IV	INITIAL CORTEX	Superior 8 Mon. Average 12 Mon. Slow 22 Mon.	Tactile understanding of the third dimension in objects which appear to be flat
III	MIDBRAIN	Superior 4 Mon. Average 7 Mon. Slow 12 Mon.	Appreciation of gnostic sensation
II	PONS	Superior 1 Mon. Average 2.5 Mon. Slow 4 Mon.	Perception of vital sensation
I	MEDULLA and CORD	Superior Birth to .5 Average Birth to 1.0 Slow Birth to 1.5	Babinski reflex

Tactile Competence

The First Developmental Level of a child's tactile competence are *skin reflexes.* There are a number of such reflexes present at birth. The Profile measures the Babinski reflex. This reflex occurs when the outside of the sole is stroked from heel to toe. The baby's big toe should flex upward and the other toes fan out.

The Second Developmental Level of a child's tactile competence is the *perception of vital sensation.* At this stage of development the baby begins to feel pain acutely and will cry if hungry or hurt in some way.

If a child has perception of vital sensation at 2.5 months, his development of tactile competence is rated *average.*

If a child has perception of vital sensation at 1 month, his development of tactile competence is rated *superior.*

If a child does *not* have perception of vital sensation until 4 months, his development of tactile competence is rated *slow.*

The Third Developmental Level of a child's tactile competence is *appreciation of gnostic sensation.* Now the baby's tactility has become more refined; he responds to more subtle sensation, such as warm versus cool.

If a baby has appreciation of gnostic sensation at 7 months, his development of tactile competence is rated *average.*

If a baby has appreciation of gnostic sensation at 4 months, his development of tactile competence is rated *superior.*

If a baby does *not* have appreciation of gnostic sensation until 12 months, his development of tactile competence is rated *slow.*

The Fourth Developmental Level of a child's tactile competence is *tactile understanding of the third dimension in objects which appear to be flat.* In other words, a penny on a table top may visually appear flat, but by touch the child can realize that it is three-dimensional.

If a child has tactile understanding of the third dimension at 12 months, his development of tactile competence is *average.*

If a child has tactile understanding of the third dimension at 8 months, his development of tactile competence is rated *superior.*

If a child does *not* have tactile understanding of the third dimension until 22 months, his development of tactile competence is rated *slow.*

The Fifth Developmental Level of a child's tactile competence is *tactile differentiation of similar but unlike objects.* In other words, he can tell, by feeling but not seeing, an apple from a ball, or a spoon from a fork.

If a child by touch alone can differentiate between similar but unlike objects at 18 months, his development of tactile competence is rated *average.*

If a child by touch alone can differentiate between similar but unlike objects at 13 months, his development of tactile competence is rated *superior.*

If a child by touch alone *cannot* differentiate between similar but unlike objects until 36 months, his development of tactile competence is rated *slow.*

The Sixth Developmental Level of a child's tactile competence is *description of objects by tactile means.* Now the child can feel objects and discern what they look like without seeing them.

 If a child can identify objects by tactile means at 36 months, his development of tactile competence is rated *average.*
 If a child can identify objects by tactile means at 22 months, his development of tactile competence is rated *superior.*
 If a child *cannot* identify objects by tactile means until 70 months, his development of tactile competence is rated *slow.*

The Seventh Developmental Level in a child's tactile competence is *tactile identification of objects using a hand consistent with hemispheric dominance.* Now the child should be able to identify almost any object within his experience by feeling it without having to look at it. Dimes, quarters, marbles, grapes, pearls, pencils, crayons, and so forth. He should consistently use his right hand if he is right-eyed, right-eared, and right-footed. Again, it makes little difference if the child is left-sided or right-sided as long as the sidedness is consistent.

 If a child can identify objects using a hand consistent with hemispheric dominance at 72 months, his development of tactile competence is rated *average.*
 If a child can identify objects using a hand consistent with hemispheric dominance at 36 months, his development of tactile competence is rated *superior.*
 If a child *cannot* identify objects using a hand consistent with hemispheric dominance until 108 months, his development of tactile competence is rated *slow.*

	BRAIN STAGE	TIME FRAME	MOBILITY
VII	SOPHISTI-CATED CORTEX	Superior 36 Mon. Average 72 Mon. Slow 108 Mon.	Using a leg in a skilled role which is consistent with the dominant hemisphere
VI	PRIMITIVE CORTEX	Superior 22 Mon. Average 36 Mon. Slow 70 Mon.	Walking and running in complete cross pattern
V	EARLY CORTEX	Superior 13 Mon. Average 18 Mon. Slow 36 Mon.	Walking with arms freed from the primary balance role
IV	INITIAL CORTEX	Superior 8 Mon. Average 12 Mon. Slow 22 Mon.	Walking with arms used in a primary balance role most frequently at or above shoulder height
III	MIDBRAIN	Superior 4 Mon. Average 7 Mon. Slow 12 Mon.	Creeping on hands and knees, culminating in cross pattern creeping
II	PONS	Superior 1 Mon. Average 2.5 Mon. Slow 4 Mon.	Crawling in the prone position culminating in cross pattern crawling
I	MEDULLA and CORD	Superior Birth to .5 Average Birth to 1.0 Slow Birth to 1.5	Movement of arms and legs without bodily movement

Mobility Competence

The First Developmental Level of a child's mobility competence is movement of arms and legs without body movement. The baby can kick and move his arms, but this movement does not propel him in any direction. This capability is present at birth.

The Second Developmental Level of a child's mobility competence is *crawling in the prone position culminating in a cross pattern.* At this stage the child begins to move about on the floor. At first the random use of arms and legs will propel the baby forward. As he gains more skill in moving, the cross pattern (right arm and left leg, then left arm and right leg) will emerge.

   If a child is crawling at 2.5 months, his development of mobility competence is rated *average.*
   If a child is crawling at 1 month, his development of mobility competence is rated *superior.*
   If a child does *not* crawl until 4 months, his development of mobility competence is rated *slow.*

The Third Developmental Level of a child's mobility competence is *creeping on hands and knees culminating in a cross pattern.* Often upon first creeping, a child moves left leg with left hand and right leg with right hand, but he should soon develop the cross pattern—left leg moving forward with right hand, right leg moving forward with left hand.

   If a child is creeping on hands and knees culminating in a cross pattern at 7 months, his mobility development is rated *average.*
   If a child is creeping on hands and knees culminating in a cross pattern at 4 months, his mobility development is rated *superior.*
   If a child is *not* creeping on hands and knees cul-

minatiṅg in a cross pattern until 12 months, his mobility development is rated *slow*.

The Fourth Developmental Level of a child's mobility competence is *walking with arms used in a primary balance role most frequently at or above shoulder height.* At this level the child uses his arms to aid his balance; he weaves back and forth, walking from one place to another. He is often called a toddler at this stage.

If a child is walking with arms in a primary balance role at 12 months, his mobility development is rated *average.*

If a child is walking with arms in a primary balance role at 8 months, his mobility development is rated *superior.*

If a child is *not* walking with arms in a primary balance role until 22 months, his mobility development is rated *slow.*

The Fifth Developmental Level of a child's mobility competence is *walking with arms freed from the primary balance role.* Now his hands have lowered, and they are not held out for help in balancing.

If a child is walking with arms freed from the primary balance role at 18 months, his mobility development is rated *average.*

If a child is walking with arms freed from the primary balance role at 13 months, his mobility development is rated *superior.*

If a child is *not* walking with arms freed from the primary balance role until 36 months, his mobility development is rated *slow.*

The Sixth Developmental Level of a child's mobility competence is *walking and running in complete cross pattern.*

Now his left hand moves forward as his right foot moves forward, and his right hand moves forward with the left foot.

If a child is walking and running in complete cross pattern at 36 months, his development is rated *average.*

If a child is walking and running in complete cross pattern at 22 months, his mobility development is rated *superior.*

If a child is *not* walking and running in complete cross pattern until 70 months, his mobility development is rated *slow.*

The Seventh Developmental Level of a child's mobility competence is *using a leg in a skilled role consistent with the dominant hemisphere* (kicking a ball, stepping up onto a stool, etc.). This is not as complicated as it sounds. If it is obvious that your child is right-handed, right-eyed, right-eared, and right-footed, then his dominant hemisphere is the left brain. Remember, the left brain controls the right side of the body, and the right brain controls the left side. If a child's dominance is developed at this level, he will consistently be right-handed, right-footed, right-eyed, and right-eared. Or he could be left-handed, left-footed, left-eyed, and left-eared. But it is important that he be *consistently* one or the other. The side is not important—the consistency is.

If a child is using a leg in a skilled role consistent with the dominant hemisphere at 72 months, his mobility development is rated *average.*

If a child is using a leg in a skilled role consistent with the dominant hemisphere at 36 months, his mobility development is rated *superior.*

If a child is *not* using a leg in a skilled role consistent with the dominant hemisphere until 108 months, his mobility development is rated *slow.*

	BRAIN STAGE	TIME FRAME	LANGUAGE
VII	SOPHISTI-CATED CORTEX	Superior 36 Mon. Average 72 Mon. Slow 108 Mon.	**Complete vocabulary and proper sentence structure**
VI	PRIMITIVE CORTEX	Superior 22 Mon. Average 36 Mon. Slow 70 Mon.	**2000 words of language and short sentences**
V	EARLY CORTEX	Superior 13 Mon. Average 18 Mon. Slow 36 Mon.	**10 to 25 words of language and two word couplets**
IV	INITIAL CORTEX	Superior 8 Mon. Average 12 Mon. Slow 22 Mon.	**Two words of speech used spontaneously and meaningfully**
III	MIDBRAIN	Superior 4 Mon. Average 7 Mon. Slow 12 Mon.	**Creation of meaningful sounds**
II	PONS	Superior 1 Mon. Average 2.5 Mon. Slow 4 Mon.	**Vital crying in response to threats to life**
I	MEDULLA and CORD	Superior Birth to .5 Average Birth to 1.0 Slow Birth to 1.5	**Birth cry and crying**

Language

The First Developmental Level of a child's language is *birth cry and crying.* This means that he cries at birth.

The Second Developmental Level of a child's language is *vital crying in response to threats to life.* In other words, the baby hears a harsh sound or is stuck by a pin, and in response he cries in a more insistent way than at the previous stage.

> If a baby has vital crying in response to threats to life at 2.5 months, his language development is rated *average.*
>
> If a baby has vital crying in response to threats to life at 1 month, his language development is rated *superior.*
>
> If a baby does *not* have vital crying in response to threats to life until 4 months, his language development is rated *slow.*

The Third Developmental Level of a child's language is *creation of meaningful sounds.* This stage goes beyond cooing and gurgling. The mother begins to realize that the baby's sounds communicate his feelings, and certain sounds become consistent.

> If a baby is creating meaningful sounds at 7 months, his language development is rated *average.*
>
> If a baby is creating meaningful sounds at 4 months, his language development is rated *superior.*
>
> If a baby is *not* creating meaningful sounds until 12 months, his language development is rated *slow.*

The Fourth Developmental Level of a child's language is *two words of speech used spontaneously and meaningfully.*

Mama, Dada, or *baba* for bottle are examples. The mother recognizes a word rather than a consistent sound. No matter what the two words are, this is a joyful level because the child has broken the code and is beginning to understand what language is.

> If a child is saying two words spontaneously and meaningfully at 12 months, his language development is rated *average*.
> If a child is saying two words spontaneously and meaningfully at 8 months, his language development is rated *superior*.
> If a child does *not* say two words spontaneously and meaningfully until 22 months, his language development is rated *slow*.

The Fifth Developmental Level of a child's language is *saying 10 to 25 words with 2-word couplets.* The couplets may be *big ball, red box,* or *Hi, Mom.* It makes little difference what the words are or in what sequence they are said; he is on his way to stringing words together sequentially.

> If a child is saying 10 to 25 words with 2-word couplets at 18 months, his language development is rated *average*.
> If a child is saying 10 to 25 words with 2-word couplets at 13 months, his language development is rated *superior*.
> If a child is *not* saying 10 to 25 words with 2-word couplets until 36 months, his language development is rated *slow*.

The Sixth Developmental Level of a child's language is *saying 2,000 words and short sentences.* Short sentences come quickly, especially the "I want a" variety. The 2,000-mark is usually reached when you find you can no longer count all of the words your child can say.

If a child can say 2,000 words and short sentences at 36 months, his language development is rated *average*.

If a child can say 2,000 words and short sentences at 22 months, his language development is rated *superior*.

If a child *cannot* say 2,000 words and speak in short sentences until 70 months, his language development is rated *slow*.

The Seventh Developmental Level of a child's language is *having a complete vocabulary and using proper sentence structure*. Now the child can ask any question and can express himself without being at a loss for words. The structure of his sentences is what we expect from others in our community. Verbally, he is now one of us.

If a child has a complete vocabulary and uses his words in proper sentence structure at 72 months, his language development is rated *average*.

If a child has a complete vocabulary and uses his words in proper sentence structure at 36 months, his language development is rated *superior*.

If a child does *not* have a complete vocabulary and does *not* use his words in proper sentence structure until 108 months, his language development is rated *slow*.

BRAIN STAGE		TIME FRAME	MANUAL COMPETENCE
VII	SOPHISTI-CATED CORTEX	Superior 36 Mon. Average 72 Mon. Slow 108 Mon.	**Using a hand to write which is consistent with the dominant hemisphere**
VI	PRIMITIVE CORTEX	Superior 22 Mon. Average 36 Mon. Slow 70 Mon.	**Bimanual function with one hand in a dominant role**
V	EARLY CORTEX	Superior 13 Mon. Average 18 Mon. Slow 36 Mon.	**Cortical opposition bilaterally and simultaneously**
IV	INITIAL CORTEX	Superior 8 Mon. Average 12 Mon. Slow 22 Mon.	**Cortical opposition in either hand**
III	MIDBRAIN	Superior 4 Mon. Average 7 Mon. Slow 12 Mon.	**Prehensile grasp**
II	PONS	Superior 1 Mon. Average 2.5 Mon. Slow 4 Mon.	**Vital release**
I	MEDULLA and CORD	Superior Birth to .5 Average Birth to 1.0 Slow Birth to 1.5	**Grasp reflex**

Manual Competence

The First Developmental Level of a child's manual competence, present at birth, is *grasp reflex*. The infant is able to tightly grasp an object placed in the palm of his hands. The grasp is maintained as long as the baby feels the pressure of the object. (Often mothers and fathers are proud of the grasp of their baby's hands, when he takes hold of his parents' fingers and does not let go. Actually, *releasing* the hand is a more sophisticated action than the ability to grasp.)

The Second Developmental Level of a child's manual competence is *vital release*. Not only can the infant take hold of an object, but he is also able to let go of it. This is a life-saving device. Before, if he had taken hold of something sharp or hot, he would not have been able to release it.

If a baby has vital release at 2.5 months, his development of manual competence is rated *average*.

If a baby has vital release at 1 month, his development of manual competence is rated *superior*.

If a baby does *not* have vital release until 4 months, his development of manual competence is rated *slow*.

The Third Developmental Level of a child's manual competence is *prehensile grasp*. Now he can pick up a larger object, such as a wooden block or a toy, by wrapping his hand around it, but he still does not use his fingers individually. It's as if he were wearing mittens.

If a baby has prehensile grasp at 7 months, his development of manual competence is rated *average*.

If a baby has prehensile grasp at 4 months, his development of manual competence is rated *superior*.

If a baby does *not* have prehensile grasp until 12 months, his development of manual competence is rated *slow*.

The Fourth Developmental Level of a child's manual competence is *cortical opposition in either hand.* In other words, he is able to press his index finger against his thumb, independent of his other three fingers. Now, by opposing his index finger to his thumb, the child can pick up a range of objects.

If a child has cortical opposition in either hand at 12 months, his development of manual competence is rated *average.*

If a child has cortical opposition in either hand at 8 months, his development of manual competence is rated *superior.*

If a child does *not* have cortical opposition in either hand until 22 months, his development of manual competence is rated *slow.*

The Fifth Developmental Level of a child's manual competence is *cortical opposition bilaterally and simultaneously.* In other words, the child now can oppose the index finger to his thumb on both hands at the same time.

If a child has cortical opposition bilaterally and simultaneously at 18 months, his development of manual competence is rated *average.*

If a child has cortical opposition bilaterally and simultaneously at 13 months, his development of manual competence is rated *superior.*

If a child does *not* have cortical opposition bilaterally and simultaneously until 36 months, his development of manual competence is rated *slow.*

The Sixth Developmental Level of a child's manual competence is *bimanual function with one hand in a dominant role.* Now the child can pour milk, sand, sugar, or even marbles from one cup into another. Here he is using both hands at the same time, coordinating an action.

If a child has bimanual function with one hand in a dominant role at 36 months, his development of manual competence is rated *average*.

If a child has bimanual function with one hand in a dominant role at 22 months, his development of manual competence is rated *superior*.

If a child does *not* have bimanual function with one hand in a dominant role until 70 months, his development of manual competence is rated *slow*.

The Seventh Developmental Level of a child's manual competence is *using a hand to write that is consistent with the dominant hemisphere*. In other words, if he is right-eared, right-eyed, and right-footed, he should also be right-handed. Again, it makes little difference whether a child is left-sided or right-sided, but both Doman and Delacato stress that a child at this stage of development should be consistent.

If a child is using a hand to write that is consistent with the dominant hemisphere at 72 months, his development of manual competence is rated *average*.

If a child is using a hand to write that is consistent with the dominant hemisphere at 36 months, his development of manual competence is rated *superior*.

If a child is *not* using a hand to write that is consistent with the dominant hemisphere until 108 months, his development of manual competence is rated *slow*.

I would imagine that by now, most mothers who have read the preceding pages have either made mental notes or have jotted notes indicating how their child's progress compares with the profile. I hope that you now have a clearer picture of the time frames your child has experienced and a better idea of what his developmental rate of speed was or is.

And I'm sure that many of you have jumped ahead of the information given and have started comparing your child's mobility with his language or his manual competence with his visual competence. Or you may have compared all six areas of development with each other. You may have found that your child's mobility is better than his language development or that his language is ahead of his manual competence. In other words, you may have found that in some areas your child is *average* while in other areas he is *superior.* And you may have found that in some areas your child is *slow.*

However, I hope that you have not concluded that that is the way it is because that is the way your child is. I hope that you have not concluded that your child excels in some areas because his "talents" lie in those areas, or that he is *average* in other areas because his "abilities" in those areas are *average.* And, of course, I hope that you have not concluded that your child is *slow* in some areas because your child is slow.

At this time, I would prefer that, instead of conclusions, you have questions. For instance:

Is my child's mobility *average* because our home environment offers him only average opportunities?

Is my child's language *slow* because his environment is not conducive to furnishing him the opportunities to encourage his speech?

If my child's language is *superior,* why is his manual competence only *average?*

Or—and these may be the most important questions:

If I alter my child's environment from an *average* one to a *superior* one, would my child's development become *superior?*

If my child is already *superior* and I make his environment even better, will he become even *more superior?*

Since my child is already *superior* in mobility and only *average* in language, if I improve his language environment, would his speech also be improved?

And now that you've asked these questions, aren't the answers obvious?

Your child's development is not necessarily a result of his genetic history or his abilities and talents, but in most cases, it is a reflection of the quality of his environment.

Now, let me make several things clear:

I am *not* saying that the child should be pressured into learning.

I am *not* saying that you should buy a desk and chair for your child's room.

I am *not,* and I repeat, *not* saying that children should be in school at an earlier age.

I am *not* saying that we should make uncaring or unfeeling mechanical geniuses of children.

I *am* saying that young children have a tremendous capacity for learning and they can learn almost without effort.

I *am* saying that young children can learn a great deal more if someone takes the time to show them the exciting things around them.

I *am* saying that young children will explore any environment around them. If that environment is exciting and rich with information, then the possibilities are great that the child will become an exciting individual and rich with information.

I *am* saying that if the environment is mediocre and average with information then the possibilities are great that the child will become mediocre and average.

I *am* saying that if the environment is dull and lacking in information, the possibilities are great that the child will grow up dull and lacking in information.

I *am* saying that there are possibilities and probabilities that by enriching a child's environment, the child's development can be accelerated.

If you tell me there are always exceptions, I will agree. But I will remind you that they *are* exceptions.

I will agree that it is possible that a child may not develop at an accelerated rate even in an enriched environment, because I know that there are such things as brain injury and other physical conditions which can restrict a child's development. It must be noted, however, that I have seen hundreds of brain-injured children develop at astonishing rates once their environments are properly programmed.

A slow child from an enriched environment is an exceptional child, but I must assert that that child is not nearly as exceptional as a superior child coming out of a dull and lacking environment. Not only do I believe this child to be rare, but he is probably nonexistent.

Without the input of information, a computer is nothing but a piece of useless machinery.

Without the input of information, a child is nothing but a living, breathing organism.

Unless a computer is programmed and in good running order, it cannot be expected to function at its fullest potential.

Unless a child is programmed and in good running order, he cannot be expected to function at his fullest potential.

If we do not respect the potential of a computer, then it is not likely to be properly programmed.

If we do not respect the potential of a child, then he is not likely to be properly programmed.

Whether or not we love a computer, it remains a computer.

Whether or not we love a child, he still may grow to become an adult. But there is little doubt that if we love him and show him our love, he will become a better human being because of the affection we give him.

If we do not love our children and do not show them our love, then they will become less than they might have been. Then we become less than we might have been.

What better way can we show children our love than by respecting their potentials and increasing their abilities?

Now I have broken the rules. I have given mothers a tool, The Doman-Delacato Developmental Profile, as a means to evaluate the development of their children. And by now, you have broken the rules and have used it. Perhaps, for the first time in your child's life, you have a clear understanding of how your child's development compares with that of other children.

I do not break rules lightly. I have a high regard for social structures and common courtesies as long as they are founded on reason. Not to drive in the wrong direction on a one-way street is a good rule. It is founded upon logic. If there was ever any logic in telling mothers not to evaluate their children's development, it escapes me.

If your evaluation of your child served no other purpose than for you to determine how he compares with other children, it has been worth the effort.

If your child's development is rated to be *superior* and you have decided to do nothing more than be pleased—well and good. That is your prerogative. I would not for one moment try to persuade you to pursue any other course.

If your child's development is rated to be *average* and you are satisfied with his being *average*—that is your business.

If your child's development is rated to be *slow* and you decide that *slow* is good enough (although I would feel a twinge of conscience and a pang of regret), I would not try to convince you to change your mind.

However, if those are your choices, now would be a good time for us to bid farewell to one another because from this point on, you may conclude that I am challenging your position. I would not want that for you. And I would not want it for me.

If you are the mother of a *slow* child and you want to make him *average,* or if you are really a dreamer and want to make him *superior,* then I suggest you do two things: 1) follow this book through to the end; and 2) get a copy of *When Children Need Help,* because chances are your child has a neurological problem.

If you are the mother of an *average* child and you would like to make him *superior*—cheers!

If you are the mother of a *superior* child and you want to make him even *more superior,* then hang in there, because that is exactly what we are about to pursue.

Chapter 9

The Most Exciting Game in Town!

Teach Your Preschooler Everything

. . . The child is curious. He wants to make sense out of things, find out how things work, gain competence and control over himself and his environment, do what he can see other people doing. He is open, receptive, and perceptive. He does not shut himself off from the strange, confused, complicated world around him. He observes it closely and sharply, tries to take it all in. He is experimental. He does not merely observe the world around him, but tastes it, touches it, hefts it, bends it, breaks it. . . .

—JOHN HOLT
How Children Learn [1]

Perhaps the final question in regard to teaching preschool children is, "What should we teach them?"

The answer for that is easier than one might surmise—
EVERYTHING *THEY* WANT TO KNOW,
and EVERYTHING *WE* WANT THEM TO KNOW!

When one becomes aware of how eager children are to learn, teaching them is much simpler than we might have supposed. And certainly, there are wide horizons and vast pieces of information from which to choose.

Teach Your Child to Read

I put reading at the top of the list because in our culture that ability probably carries more weight than any other in providing the options and choices a person will have while a student, and as an adult. If we lived in the jungle, perhaps number one on the list would be, teach your child to throw a spear. But our jungles are ones of concrete and paper, of xerox copies and typewritter ribbons, of computerized statistics and newsprint. Our weapons are receptive minds and the ability to analyze printed matter.

In Chapter 4, we discussed the whys and the hows to teach your child to read.

How to Choose a Book for a Preschooler

Most books for children who are under five years of age are awful. They are composed on the premise that children love fantasies. However, the opposite is probably the case—adults love fantasies. Therefore they offer the gingerbread man and cartoon animals to their little ones. What harm is there in showing children flying elephants and foxes walking around dressed as people? None at all if we present these stories as fantasies and try not to fool the kid into believing that all of these things actually exist.

The assumption seems to be that little kids think fairy tales are terribly interesting and that realities are boring. The foolhardiness of such assumptions is underwhelming, for the assumptions are wrong. Children are fascinated with *everything* around them. And the "realer" those things are, the more interesting they become.

What fairy tale is as fascinating as how bees make honey?

What fantasy is as exhilarating as the activity of an anthill?

What tall tale is as entertaining as a caterpillar spinning a cocoon?

What is more dazzling than a lightning bug flickering in the summer's night?

How many do I have to name for you to get the idea?

If you want to show your child a miracle, plant a tiny seed in a pot of dirt and let him watch it grow, day by day. Not only are you showing him a miracle in your own home, but you are teaching him agriculture.

It is not my intention to try to put the children's books publishers out of business. In fact, I wish there were more and better children's books published. The attitudes of the people involved in producing materials are schizophrenic to say the least. Many of the editors insist that the story line be simple, simple, simple, and then they allow some artist to fill the pages with visual chaos—stylized bears, distorted backgrounds, garish colors, cartoon people, and so on. Most of the editors I talk with readily admit that although they hope children will enjoy them, most books are designed basically to catch the attention of adults. So they insist that the illustrations must look like what the adults think would entertain children. If that is not selling products by devious means, I don't know what is.

When selecting a book for your preschooler, pick one that has good, accurate information in it. Make sure the illustrations are large and well defined and that the stories contain good learning experiences. In the first books you buy, be sure the dogs look like dogs and the cows look like cows. Mickey Mouse is just as much fun after the child knows what a real mouse looks like. Don't confront him with clutter that he has to sort out. First show him what the real world is like and then show him the cartoons and the stylizations. Kids aren't really turned on by the cutesy pictures. It's the parents' "oohs" and "ahs" that the kid really enjoys. If you *ooh* over a picture of a real tiger, your kid will dig that picture just as much, if not more so, than he would some striped cartoon thing. It's the time spent looking at books with you that he loves, not the printed page. You are his guide. He loves to be interested in the things which you find fun and thrilling.

It is not my design to put down Dr. Seuss or Walt Disney or to deprive little children of the pleasure of *The Cat in the Hat* or Donald Duck. Because they are such fun, children are going to see these things anyway. But what has happened is that children have been fed a daily visual and auditory diet of fantasy and have been given so few learning experiences of substance. I'm not saying *delete,* I'm saying *broaden* the spectrum of materials. However, if one or the other has to wait, show your child Gainsborough first. Let Goofy and his friends stand in line.

In selecting books to show or read to your preschooler, you must sift and sort, for to my knowledge, there is no one complete set that will introduce your child to his environment. The *Tell Me Why* books are very good, but they would be even better if the illustrations were larger and more realistic. Some of the Childcraft books are excellent, especially the one entitled *Look Again.*

Most adult picture books beat kids' books hands down. Go to the library and borrow some history of art books—the encyclopedia types with large color reproductions. Better still, buy your own and begin a library. Show your child the finest—El Greco, Vermeer, Michaelangelo, Da Vinci—and for real fantasy and imagination, some Dali.

Incidentally, when you're showing your child these books, don't feel compelled to skip over the pictures of nudity. Unless you have already instilled in the child that the human form is obscene and should be hidden, he will not be shocked at all. In fact, he will find them quite interesting. And why shouldn't he? After all, you're showing him information about his own species. In school that might be called an anatomy lesson, but at home, it can very well be labeled pertinent information.

Children think that breasts and penises are no more or no less interesting than are noses or ears or belly buttons. And their questions do not mean that you are about to be asked for explicit information about the facts of life. Answer the questions they ask. Don't jump in feet first and begin to anticipate that they want to know more than their questions require.

"What's that?"

"That's the man's penis."

"Do all people have one?"

"Only men."

"Women don't?"

"No, they do not."

"Does Daddy have one?"

"Yes."

"But you don't?"

"That's right. I don't because I'm a woman."

"Why?"

And never be afraid to give this answer, because children quickly learn to accept it: "Because that's the way it is."

That's a very good answer. Some parents may prefer to say, "Because that's the way God made us." And there's certainly nothing wrong with that approach. As long as the child doesn't have the idea that bodies are something to be ashamed of, such an answer doesn't get either you or God into trouble.

"What are those?"

"They're breasts. Women have those when they grow up."

"Why?"

"Because when they have babies, their breasts fill with milk and they can feed them."

"Don't men have breasts?"

"Yes, but they are not as large and they don't fill with milk."

"Why?"

"Because that's the way it is."

Simple and nice. No taboos have been broken and the child has been given good pieces of information. It should be obvious that the young child does not come to the conclusion that genitals should be covered or hidden unless we tell him that either verbally or by our actions. And why should he? Certainly in his early years, his or hers aren't private secrets. No baby grabs a cloth to cover himself when his parents change his diaper or prepare him for his bath. In fact, it's not until he gets older and adults tell him that he mustn't "streak" across the front yard or pull his pants down when company is in the house that he becomes confused by the changing rules.

Whether parents walk around the house in their birthday suits or not is an argument I leave for the psychiatrists and your personal preference. On second thought, I would rather leave that decision to you, because if you wait for the psychiatrists to agree on anything, it will probably be too late for your child. By that time he may be facing senility, whiling away his remaining years.

Teach Your Child to Write

The better your child can communicate his thoughts and his feelings, the better he will relate to his present and future environments. We've discussed ways to teach him to write in Chapter 4.

Teach Your Child to Speak Clearly

If you and the other members of your family speak clearly, your child probably will. Remember, you are programming his brain. If all he hears are mumbles and dropped consonants, that's the way he is likely to talk. If you want him to speak baby talk then you *gitchy-goo* him until his eyes cross. But if you want him to communicate as a person, then demonstrate how grown people speak.

Talk to your child from the time he is born. "While I cannot guarantee that your child will develop good understanding if you talk to him," says Gretchen Kerr, director of the Children's Institute, "I *can* guarantee that he will *not* develop understanding if you do *not* talk to him."[2]

Teach Your Child to Verbalize His Feelings

This too is learned by example. Children who grow up in families where members rarely express their emotions seldom express their feelings. If you want your child to share his emotions with you then you must first share some of yours with him. In the past, girls have been programmed to express their emotions more than boys have. ("Men don't cry" and all that nonsense.) But we're getting away from that today. If we teach children to express themselves more openly when they are young, there's a good chance that years later they won't wind up sprawled out on an analyst's couch, wringing their hands and biting their lips.

Teach Your Child to Touch

If you own a playpen, throw it away! Better still, make kindling out of it. If you only discard it, someone else might find it and cage some other child. If you don't have one, good for you! Better yet, good for your child. Being caged behind bars is a lousy way for a kid to first view the world you brought him into.

Allow your child the freedom to navigate throughout the house. If you have a priceless Ming vase or breakable decorations, put them away until he's trustworthy. Also get all poisons and potential dangers well out of his reach.

Encourage him to touch and feel all the things around him —tables, chairs, curtains, cups, saucers, the rug, the floor, walls, sculpture—everything. All of these things are information. I realize that by allowing him such freedom, you must constantly be aware of where he is and what he is doing, but this time quickly passes.

Teach Him About His Environment

Acquaint him with his own yard and immediate neighborhood.

Even if at first he doesn't respond to everything you say to him, give him names for everything. Let him feel the grass and leaves and flowers. In the warmer months, spend as much time outside as you both enjoy. Let him feel the soil and sand and rocks. Show him butterflies and ants and caterpillars.

Explore your yard with him. Show him what his neighborhood is like. Take walks with him. Draw his attention to landmarks and directions. Sometimes mothers hesitate to take their small children out of their own yards because they fear it will encourage them to set out on explorations of their own. Most children are eager to try this anyway. However, should they stray from you, the better acclimated they are with their own neighborhood, the more likely they are to find their way home. Obviously everything you do with your child requires certain amounts of precaution.

Neighborhoods are as individual as are the people who inhabit them. The atmosphere can be friendly, cordial, and pleasant or it can be one of barriers, hostility, and danger. Sometimes within a city block, one finds strange combinations of passive hostility, friendly fortification, and obvious peril. The midtown ghettos do not have exclusive claim to any of these combinations. One can find the same ingredients in the neighborhood atmosphere of the concrete jungle or in the two-car garage, manicured-lawn settings of suburbia.

It is obvious that the environment in impoverished areas, both rural and urban, greatly reduces the developmental potential of the children therein. The damage to these children can be both physical and mental. When stated in terms of thousands, the individual tragedies become lost in numbers. The tragedy becomes significant only if one of these children is *my* child or *your* child.

While I feel a loss for the child in the ghetto, I also have sympathy for the child in the suburbs. I think someone should write a book about the culturally deprived child in the suburbs—the child who rides everywhere he goes in the back of a station wagon. This child is not allowed to walk to the corner grocery on his own because there is no corner grocery. This child is not allowed to navigate the backyards and alleyways because of chain-link fences and costly shrubbery. This child is not allowed by public ordinance to build a tree house. In many ways, his surroundings are as sterile as the ghetto is chaotic.

Whatever your neighborhood is like, from a very early age, acquaint your child with its geography, attitudes, and advantages, and also make him aware of the dangers, whether those threats are physical or emotional.

Teach Your Child to Be Creative

If you are creative, he will certainly want to be. Several ways of encouraging his creativity are given in Chapter 6.

Teach Your Child Mathematic Concepts

Once he gets the idea of one and two and three, don't stop at ten. Show him groups of things and tell him the number. If children are shown large groups of things and told the amount, they can very quickly visualize them. It's what Glenn Doman calls *instant mathematics.* At The Institutes, mothers of brain-injured children are told to paste large red dots in random scatterings on flashcards and tell the child the number. I have seen three-year-old children who can instantly tell which card has eighty-two dots on it, or ninety-six, or one hundred and one. Remember, your child's brain is growing so fast that it will record vast amounts of information much easier and quicker than yours will. You will probably have to count the dots or objects in lots of fourteen or more, but your child can learn to recognize them with little effort.

Other approaches have been discussed in Chapter 6.

Teach Your Child to Be an Athlete

Encourage him to tumble and run and do all the things that require physical coordination. In Penfield, New York, there is a program called "Fit By Five," developed by the nationally known diving coach, Betty Perkins, where preschoolers are taught gymnastics. In Australia, Claire Timmermans shows mothers how to teach their babies to swim. Claire's book, *How to Teach Your Baby to Swim,* has recently been published in this country. Illustrated with many pictures, it's one of the best how-to books I've ever encountered.

Certainly circus people have always had the right idea. Their children are taught acrobatics at very early ages. If you play tennis, teach your child. If you are a dancer, teach your child. If you ride horses, teach your child. If you are not athletic, find people who are and give them the privilege of teaching your child.

Teach Your Child the Rules of Safety

Make him aware of signs and streetlights. Caution him about broken glass, knives, etc. Everything you see that might endanger him show to him, before you pick them up and get them out of his way. Give him the information.

Teach Him to Be Sociable

Have friends in your home and take him to other people's homes from a very early age. On the first trips, be sure that you concentrate on his being comfortable rather than on your visit. Don't spend your time saying "no" to him all the while you are there. Make the first outings short and for his benefit, not for yours. He will soon learn what things he is allowed to touch and those he is not.

At first, his playtime with other children should be in short segments of time. Don't fool yourself that he is going to learn a lot from children his own age. He'll learn more from older children and you than he'll learn from his peer group. Chances are he will learn some wrong information and bad habits from them too. (We'll go into this in more detail in the next chapter.)

Teach Your Child to Be Imaginative

Don't buy toys that wind up and perform their total repertoire in one minute, and then repeat the same action over and over. How many times have you heard a parent say, "I don't know what's the matter with that kid. He's got a box full of toys and he never plays with them." Or, "Boy, he's sure got a short attention span." In most cases, a child can learn anything and everything possible about a new toy in a few minutes. As Glenn Doman says, "He'll look at it, touch it, smell it, shake it, listen to it, and taste it. The only thing left for him to learn from it is will it break."

Cardboard boxes are great toys because they can become anything—a little house, a car, a rocket ship, and better still, they can be all of these things whenever the child changes his mind and turns them in a different direction.

Teach Your Child the Difference Between the Real and the Unreal

Whether adults like to admit it or not, they are habitual liars to little children. During their early years we tell children the damnedest nonsense and laugh at them when they believe our outrageous stories.

"Storks bring babies."

"Be good, or the Boogie Man will get you."

"A little bird told me so."

"The tooth fairy will come in the night."

"The sandman will slip into your bedroom."

"Children who ask too many questions grow long noses."

Then, of course, there are Santa Claus, the Easter Bunny, and all of the other myths adults delight in perpetuating. We tell ourselves that since children cannot tell the difference between fantasy and truth, and since they believe anything and everything we tell them, it doesn't hurt to lie to them. We have convinced ourselves that fantasies are a part of childhood and that children enjoy them so. It is fair to question, though, whether children enjoy the fairy tales as much as adults delight in confusing their little heads.

Does this mean that I am out to murder Santa Claus and the tooth fairy? No, I am not. Because I am an adult, and as an adult, I still believe in Santa Claus and fairies—they are delightful illusions. But it should be apparent that these illusions are really delusions. Most adults remember that black day when they learned that Santa Claus was really a charge account at Montgomery Ward and that Dad ate the cookies left by the fireplace for St. Nick. And most of us recall with a sad pang that first Christmas without the excitement of listening for the sound of reindeer hooves on the roof.

During children's early years we tell them all of these myths and cross our hearts and swear that they are true. In later years, when they find that we have "storied" to them, is it small wonder that they begin to question many things we have told them? Perhaps children learn the difference between white lies and black lies, but they certainly have earned the right to question whether or not adults know the difference.

If we view the brain as a computer, which it clearly is, then shouldn't we become more cautious about the information we feed into it? Of course we should.

During a special lecture to a group of scientists, Glenn Doman told them that before the age of five a child's brain will indiscriminately accept any information as fact. He told them that computer experts have a beautiful anonym— "Gigo"—"Garbage in—garbage out." Computer experts know that if wrong information is placed into a computer, one can expect wrong information to come out. In order to receive proper information from the computer the wrong information must be cancelled. Doman stressed that the same is true with human beings—that if wrong information is given to a child before he is five years of age, for the rest of his life, he has to cancel erroneous concepts before he can utilize a corrected fact.

The scientists took exception to Doman's statement and questioned its validity. So Doman said, "Let me ask you a question and you tell me the first answer that comes to your minds." Then he asked, "What is the moon made of?"

The room was soon filled with the scientists' laughter. They were convinced. Although some of the men present were employed in space exploration projects and had the most recent data in regard to the composition of the moon, the first answer that came to their minds was—*"green cheese."*

We do not purposely intend to lie to children. But we do it anyway. Sometimes we lie because we believe they could not understand a certain piece of information even if we told them. And sometimes we lie as a cover-up because we really do not know the answer ourselves. The main reason we continue to lie to them is that we have so little respect for them as individuals and so little regard for their potentials.

As Doman told the scientists, no matter how they would like to cancel that wrong piece of information from their brains, there is no way they can do it because before they were five years old, a well-meaning Aunt Sue or Uncle Joe programmed their brains with "green cheese." Now, for the rest of their lives, they will have to cancel that falsity before they can sort out facts.

Once we begin to look at the brain as a computer, then we begin to look at infants differently. We begin to see them not as little ignorant blobs, but we begin to realize that they are innocent and unprogrammed human beings. The real challenge we should understand is that each child has the potential of whatever we program him to be.

One adult to another, would I tell you outrageous lies? Of course not. Everyone knows it's immoral to lie to adults. But show us a kid, and we can delight in telling him the whiffiest pieces of nonsense he has ever heard. Everyone knows it is a lot of fun to spoof children. Most adults do it. What a pity! But no matter how much fun the lie may be, compared to giving a child accurate information it could hardly be regarded as even a minor achievement.

If you want to show your child animals, let him see what the real ones look like. I hate to suggest that you take him to a zoo, unless your city has the kind with open areas where the animals can move about as freely as possible. Avoid the confined cage kind as you would the plague. Showing a child a caged animal is not showing him the animal at all. A lion pacing back and forth in a nine by twelve enclosure is no more representative of a real lion than a mental patient is of a real person. We would not take children to a mental hospital and have them walk from room to room so they could see what real people look like, now would we? Then why would we want to show them brain-injured, environmentally deprived animals? It would be better to take them to a park and let them see what real squirrels are like or into the backyard and show them real, alive, functioning ants and bees and spiders. If you do take them to a zoo, the best lesson you can teach them is how terrible it is to cage any living thing.

Children learn by facts not by illusion. When touring a zoo, adults imagine the lions and the tigers roaming the African savannahs. But kids see exactly what they see. And they hear what they hear. And they smell what they smell. The stench in most zoos is nauseating. For the sake of showing the kids, adults try to ignore the odors and view as many cages as possible from upwind. But kids don't block out the odors. They smell it like it is and often conclude that animals are dirty, smelly things.

When our son was about five years old, we took him on a tour through the city zoo. As we were driving home, I asked, "Todd, what did you think of the zoo?"

"It's like a paradise restroom," he answered.

Several nights during the week there are some very good shows on television—"Wild Kingdom" and the Disney nature shows to name two. Don't insist that your child sit still and watch them as if he were studying for a college exam. Simply arrange your time so that during those shows you can sit down and display that these things are interesting to you. Be available to answer his questions. If he becomes distracted, be ready to shift your interest too. Allow him the freedom to explore. Perhaps he suddenly wonders how his rocking chair is constructed or he notices the print on your dress or the color of a bowl on the coffee table. Why should you think that the pictures and sounds on television are more interesting than these?

Don't ever think that a child has to give any one thing his undivided attention. Adults with their slow-thinking, slow-learning old brains may have to plod along to learn, but a three-year-old with his fast-growing, fast-absorbing young brain can quickly learn unrelated pieces of information. Don't slow him down to your pace or try to teach him with unyielding schedules.

Give Your Child Every Opportunity to Learn!

Give your child every opportunity to do things for himself even though it takes him longer or inconveniences you.

If he has difficulty in learning to tie shoe laces, get a

clothesline rope and show him how to tie it in a bow.

If at first modeling clay is difficult for him to mold into balls, make some bread dough and show him how to make balls of it and place them in a muffin pan.

Show him how to use a rolling pin with the dough or with graham or soda crackers. It may be a bit messy but you are teaching him what tools are for.

In the summer show him how to dig holes with a hand shovel. Let him start when the earth is soft, even if you have to prepare an area of soil the day before.

Build him a sand box big enough for him to play in—not one of those little four-foot square, prefabricated jobs which are packaged for easy assembly, but build one that covers an eight-foot square area. During warm weather let him play in it, wearing the least amount of clothing possible so he has the opportunity to feel the world around him.

Let him go barefoot in and out of the house as much as possible so his feet have direct contact with the surfaces under his feet. Be sure to remove broken glass, sharp rocks, etc., from any area he might have to cross.

Give him the chance to snap greenbeans, shell peas, stir cake icing with a big spoon, and let him graduate to using hand-operated egg beaters.

If pouring milk is a spill problem, fill a cup with dried peas, beans, or rice and let him pour them from one cup to another. Or fill the cup with raisins or puffed rice and add the incentive that he may eat what is not spilled. Let him progress to thick liquids such as ketchup, honey, molasses, corn syrup, etc.

Give the child the opportunity to learn and experience the difference between hard and soft, smooth and rough, hot and cold.

Play games with swatches of different materials—silk, carpeting, burlap, satin, corduroy, linoleum, sandpaper. Hand him those objects under the table or behind his back so he can learn to identify them without looking.

Vary the temperature of bath water, from cool to warm

and from warm to cool, so he has more opportunity to experience differences in total body sensations. Dry him briskly with a nubby towel.

Fathers love to hold children up in the air and roughhouse with them. Encourage this type of play, holding the child upside down, swinging him so that he has the chance to feel the changes of gravity force.

Give the child the opportunity to experience extremes in tastes—salty, sweet, sour, bitter—and prepare different textured foods, and even though it may be a messy procedure, encourage him to fill his own plate and select his own food by name.

To help him develop the perception of smells, open spice cans, one by one. Prepare high-intensity odor foods, such as onions or cabbage and let him smell them cooking. Even though it takes extra time, prepare one of these things ahead of the rest of the dinner so he has the opportunity to smell one odor rather than the accumulated smells of dinner.

Buy finger paints—yes, they are messy, but they provide complete hand sensations.

Give your child a dust cloth and let him dust tables, shelves, books.

Take some books out of the bookcase and let him put them back.

Let him tear construction paper of different colors into pieces and show him how to paste the pieces on a large sheet of paper. Show him different colors and shapes, so he can recognize them by name.

Show him how to use blunt-nosed scissors and let him cut favorite pictures out of old magazines.

When you take him to the supermarket, let him prepare a list of things to find. Show him how to write them, even if with large crayons on a big piece of paper. Who says that a shopping list has to be on the back of an envelope?

Buy a miniature rake and let him help in the yard. Let him graduate to the big one as soon as he can.

Invent toys that excite his imagination instead of buying

toys that are what they are and have no potential for being anything else.

If at first, stacking small wooden blocks is a problem for your preschooler, save empty cereal boxes, soap boxes, shoe boxes, etc., to use for building towers, bridges, or whatever.

Show him how to separate things into sets of twos and threes, two big boxes, three small ones, etc. Let him find mates of shoes, socks, and mittens.

Let the child help sort the laundry and show him how to fold the washcloths and towels. Give him the opportunity to carry them and stack them on the shelf. Children love to be helpers.

If your child has trouble catching a beachball, play catch with a pillow and let him graduate to catching a bean bag. If he falls down when the pillow hits him, stuff a pillow with lighter-weight material, but don't fill it completely full; then gradually add more stuffing to it.

You won't have to encourage your child to scatter miniature toys on the floor, but play a pick-up game with him. For variety—and to develop additional balance skills—have him pick the objects up with his toes.

Give him the opportunity to listen for specific sounds—the stove timer, the alarm clock, etc.

Have friends and relatives call him often and talk to him on the telephone. Show him how to dial numbers.

Give your child the opportunity to set the table for lunch —use plastic plates if you're not up to a lot of excitement. Show him how to use measuring cups and spoons.

Take him on bus trips, to restaurants, and various sites of interest, such as fire stations, observatories, parks, etc.

In other words, be inventive. For each one of the activities I have mentioned, you can probably think of a thousand others.

Discipline Your Child

Although discipline is extremely important in the development of a child, I wouldn't venture to tell you how to discipline yours except to mention: Use all the patience you can muster, all the love you have to give, and all the reasoning you can discern.

However, I notice that parents who are actively interested in their children and reward their curiosity with meaningful learning experiences often have less need for disciplinary measures than parents who ignore their children until they get into mischief.

Respect Your Child

This may appear to be a strange piece of advice. Too often the word "love" is confused with the word "respect." However, they are not at all the same. I wouldn't dare be so presumptuous as to suggest to parents that they should love their child. Such a suggestion implies that if they were not told to do so, the idea might never occur to them. Parents who love their children love them without such suggestions, and those who don't wouldn't understand it even if the words were engraved on their foreheads.

Yet, we sometimes forget to respect our children. Like adults, children are eager to accomplish goals and they enjoy being rewarded for achievements. You are the expert in regard to your child. You know best when your child has functioned at the highest extent of his abilities. When he does, don't wait—praise him. "Oohs" and "ahs" are great sound effects, and hugs and kisses are better than any blue ribbon. If you reward him and show him that you respect him for his achievements, you will see his abilities grow and broaden. Nurture him and encourage him as if his life depends upon your evaluations and your command of his early years—for indeed it does!

Said the poet Kahlil Gibran, "You are the bows from which your children as living arrows are sent forth."[3]

Teach Your Child Good Nutritional Habits

The best way to teach a child proper nutrition is by letting him experience healthy foods. Your child learns to eat and enjoy those foods which you prepare. If you supply him with potato chips and candy he will learn what it's like to have a mouthful of cavities, digestive problems, and a loss of energy. But if you provide him with proper nutrients, he learns what a healthy body feels like and how it functions.

In recent years, snack food drive-ins and sugar-coated cereal pushers have amassed fortunes by making their products so accessible and seductive (85 percent of the popularly advertised, sugar-coated cereals are classified as candy by U.S. Department of Agriculture standards). In many ways, they are as threatening as the dope-peddling junkie because they are helping to undermine children's health by encouraging their addiction to french-fried and sugar-processed pap. While the taste of such froth may be a treat for the palate, the consumption is a dire threat to the health of children and adults alike.

Instead, educate your child's taste to include health-building foods:

Avoid refined sugar (white and brown), and *all* refined sugar products. Substitute unprocessed honey and molasses.

Refrain from using *all* refined flour products. Begin using whole-grain, stone-ground flours (and breads made with them), which have not been robbed of vital nutrients during overprocessing. Delicious breads and pastries can be home-baked with whole-grain flours and honey or molasses.

In lieu of refined, presweetened and sugar-coated cereals, serve whole-grain products such as whole wheat, brown rice, and rolled oats.

Serve moderate amounts of low-fat meat, fish, and poultry

(baked, not fried), and give your family *fresh* fruits and vegetables, raw or barely cooked.

At snack time, avoid "trash" foods. Accustom your child to eating fresh or dried fruits, nuts, raisins, popcorn, sunflower seeds, carrot and celery sticks, and whole-grain pretzels. Forget soft drinks and watered-down, presweetened, artificially flavored fruit drinks. Serve *pure* fruit juices instead.

If you are concerned about your family's nutrition, I highly recommend that you read *Let's Have Healthy Children* by nutritionist, Adelle Davis, and Dr. David Reuben's recent book, *The Save Your Life Diet.* Both authors warn of the dangers of the highly refined, overly processed, chemically preserved foods constituting the bulk of the typical American diet.

Nutritionally sound or unsound eating patterns are established during the child's early years, and most likely will be maintained through his life. If you want your child to function at his maximum potential then give him the proper nutrients. Remember, you have a Cadillac kid—don't fill him up with Model T fuels.

Whether your child is male or female, show him (or her) how to prepare foods. The idea that only girls need to know how to cook is ridiculous. Boys have to eat too, and most boys, at some time during their lives, have to select and prepare their own food. There is certainly nothing sissy about frying an egg or washing the pan.

I'm sure, after reading these suggestions, that most mothers will have two thoughts burst into their heads: 1) "Such a program would take up the entire day." And 2) "Wouldn't you know these suggestions are made by a man."

Let's look at the second thought first. If you think that most fathers could not initiate such a program, I would agree wholeheartedly. But I am convinced that if they want to, most mothers can. From the enormous amounts of mail Glenn Doman receives from mothers who have taught their preschoolers everything from reading to swimming, it is clearly evident that thousands have already accomplished this quite successfully.

Teaching your preschooler does take time, but not the entire day—only segments during the day. As you'll see, when you get *The Doman Reading Kit,* you can teach your child to read using no more than fifteen minutes a day. The other things you add only encompass a few minutes at a time, and these are scattered throughout the hours. You make the schedule. Better still, don't make a schedule. Let your child's responses influence your timetable. If the things you are teaching him are interesting and fun, he will urge you to find time to teach him more.

Perhaps the most difficult aspect of teaching your child will be to adapt the routine of your day to his peak interest time. If he's eager to paint at nine o'clock in the morning, leave the dishes in the sink and get out the easel and brushes. If he is eager to read at ten o'clock, turn off the vacuum cleaner and get out the word cards. If you are talking on the phone and he asks you a question, excuse yourself from the adult on the line and answer his query. The adult can wait, but that question may never again be as important to your child. The floor that needs waxing will still be there after your child is grown, but you can never recapture his early years.

Can you do it? If you want to, I am convinced that you can. When our son was on the therapy program for eighteen months, that program engulfed ten hours of each and every day. There were eye exercises, mobility programs, reading programs, and so on. During the course of those months we had over 130 volunteers who came into our home to help pattern his mobility. Twelve people came each day. Not only did Nancy have most of the responsibility for teaching Todd, but she also had to coordinate people. She was very successful in doing both, and the result was that she turned a brain-injured child into a normal child.

Today there are thousands of mothers who are successfully doing the same thing. Time and again when we talk to them, we find that they do not ask for ways to lessen their job; instead they pray for longer days and more things to do to accelerate their children's abilities.

The time required for you to alter the development of your well child, compared to the hours and the days and the years needed to make a brain-injured child well, is infinitesimal.

Remember the answer Glenn Doman gave to the mothers who wrote, "I noticed that when my child learned to read that his physical coordination improved" or "her hearing improved" or "his speech improved." "Is there any connection between the two . . . or three . . . or four?"

He answered, "Everything we do to alter the function of the brain has the potential to alter the other functions." He illustrates this beautifully by saying, "There seems to be a string connecting all human functions. If one is improved, then it seems to pull the others up with. If a child's manual competence is improved, his speech improves. If his visual competence is improved, his mobility improves, and so on. All functions are interrelated. And why should that surprise us? Aren't they all coordinated by the brain? And if we improve the child's brain function in one area, doesn't it stand to reason that we are also affecting other areas of the brain at the same time? Of course it does."

I have given you a list of dos. Although I dislike don'ts, there is one I feel I must offer. During any of these activities in which mother and child or father and child are engaged, *don't* tell your child that he is "playing school." For you are *not* playing at all. You are showing your child some necessary steps of development to survive in our modern society.

Children want to learn as much, if not more, as they want to play. Most important of all, enjoy showing your child how to do new and exciting things. You enjoy him and he will enjoy you.

The game is called *Teach Your Preschooler Everything!* It's the most exciting game in town!

Chapter 10

Should You Send
Your Preschooler to a Preschool
or a Day-Care Center?

*This Program Was Prerecorded
Before It Was Recorded*

Let's get right to the point.

Should you send your preschooler to a preschool or a day-care center?

Only if your other choices are leaving him in a lion's cage, a shark-infested surf, or a burning building.

I don't like to play word games. I have a disdain for the name "day-care center" because its title implies that this is a place where children are physically taken care of during the day—where they are fed, clothed, and watched while their parents are at work or somewhere else. Nothing in the title suggests that while there, the child will be taught anything. "Preschool" bothers me in a different way, because it infers that it is a school where children go before they go to school. The term is reminiscent of the television tagline, "this program was prerecorded." How can you prerecord something something before you record it?

While things are not always as they sound, quite often they are worse. Of course, all the institutions that care for children during the day could change their names to learning centers, but that would not, automatically, make them learning centers.

If anyone believes that day-care centers and preschools were primarily initiated to benefit children, he should flush that piece of tripe out of his head immediately. These places have sprouted like dandelions in a summer's lawn for the convenience of adults.

The attitude of appeasing adults isn't new to the world. It's always been that way. If there is a question of benefiting children or conveniencing adults, the big people have always had their way.

In his book *Centuries of Childhood,* Phillippe Aries reminds us that although adults like to pretend that the child labor laws were compassionate ones brought into effect to keep innocent little children out of the factories and mines, in reality, those laws were devised to eliminate them as competition with the big people in obtaining and maintaining jobs.

There are four main reasons why children are sent to day-care centers and preschools:

•Mothers have no choice but to work and they have no other place to send their children.

•Mothers would rather work than stay home.

•Mothers regard their children as interferences in their activities.

•Mothers believe that group experience activities are good for their children, and that teachers can teach them more than they can learn at home.

Mothers who have no choice but to work, have no choice. It's as simple as that. Sad to say, it is usually those mothers who also have fewer choices as to the quality of the places they must leave their children. Customarily, they must settle on the place nearest their homes. They are grateful if the establishment is clean and hope that while there, their children aren't physically hurt or allowed to be lonely. Most often, they have no way to insist that the child be taught anything more than to wait in line and keep his hands to himself.

Mothers who would rather work than stay home with their children are often better off financially and have more choices of the kind of places they leave their children. The fee for the child's care usually comes out of their paycheck, easing their consciences somewhat. Too often these women little realize the importance of those early years. They have been advised into numbness that children should wait until they enter school before learning anything really important. We have seen in this writing how detrimental and damaging such advice can be.

Mothers who consider their children nuisances and caring for them to be a bore, may have been worn into the same numbness by the do-nothing advice. Frequently though, when mothers commence to teach their children and find out how exciting it is, they often cancel the bridge clubs and luncheons. Others are bored wherever they are, but these women aren't bored mothers—they are bored women who happen to be mothers. Out of all the groups, possibly their children will profit more from a day-care center or a preschool, because, for a child, there is nothing less rewarding than sitting home with a bored keeper.

Mothers who think that sending their children to a day-care center or a preschool is a "far, far better thing than they have ever done," haven't read this book.

Who Says Children Learn Better in Herds?

Some friends of mine in New York City strongly object to these negative opinions on day-care centers and preschools. They argue that such conclusions are drawn from the situation of an upper-middle-class suburban neighborhood, and with no regard for urban dwellers.

My friends are parents of a preschooler who attends a preschool. However, the mother maintains that even if she did not work, she would enroll her child in a *good* preschool because children who live in apartments have so little opportunity to be with other children. They maintain that, for the urban child, there is a need for places where he can be with other children. They contend that a basic facet of his adjustment to his peers is neglected if he is surrounded only by adults.

Although I agree that children do learn things from their peers they would not learn from adults, not all of the pieces of information they share are either good or accurate. And it is highly questionable whether a child can learn as much from other children as he can from adults.

I have observed that my own children brought massive amounts of wrong information home from play. Much of the wrong information about sex was given to them on the authority of neighborhood children. Did you know that a girl can get pregnant if a boy puts his finger in her navel? Or did you know that some boys' penises have eyes?

I would not argue for one minute that children do not receive false information from adults as well. Of course they do. Not only do adults pass on errors in judgment and incorrect knowledge to children, but sometimes they lie in order to avoid answering questions honestly. However, the point is, fact for fact, children can get more accurate information from adults than they can from other children.

I agree that seeing children together is a happy sight. And we do have this idea, whether it's right or not, that like kinds enjoy being together. But why stick them in classrooms, away from everyday activities? In thinking back, I fondly remember summer afternoons of climbing trees and building forts with children in my neighborhood. I would like for all children to have the experiences of racing tricycles and spitting in the streets. Classrooms certainly don't provide those opportunities.

The argument is also raised that preschools prepare children for real school. That's like preparing children for measles by giving them the measles.

What can children learn at preschool that they can't learn at home much better and much easier? I suppose they can learn to stand in line and wait their turn. They can learn to raise their hands before speaking. They can learn what it's like to be away from home at an earlier age. And they learn that the teacher is the boss. If there is anything else they can learn that they can't learn at home, it escapes me. And surely it doesn't require much time to learn those. As quickly as preschoolers can learn, they don't have to be regimented for three or six hours a day, five days a week to learn what institutional life is like.

And what about Montessori schools? They are as good as the people who run them. Some are excellent. Some are mediocre. And some are dull as kraut. Their appearances can be misleading. With stacks of colored materials and gadgets, they often appear more exciting than they really are.

If you want your child to be initiated into group settings, Sunday School offers such an opportunity. Best of all, those classes are available only once a week so they often seem like a treat rather than a jail sentence.

As we have seen, mothers have the abilities to teach their children vast amounts of information. It is doubtful that one teacher with twenty to thirty youngsters in her charge could even come close to teaching a child as much as can an eager mother on a one-to-one basis.

In her article "Do You Know How to Play with Your Child?" Betty Hannah Hoffman reports this statement made by Dr. Glen Nimnicht, a leading educational psychologist, responsible for training *Head Start* and *Follow Through* teachers throughout the United States: "The early years are crucial in the development of a child's potential, . . . It's my hunch that twenty minutes a day playing with his mother does a pre-schooler as much good as three hours in a class-room."[1]

Upon looking around us, we can readily see that practically all of our institutions are failing miserably. Our judicial systems and prisons aren't detering crimes in our streets. Our schools are failing to teach over thirty percent of their students to read on grade level. Numerous officials of our government have been involved in illegal pursuits. Nursing homes for the elderly are front-page scandals.

If we listed the failures of all the institutions, we would fill pages with depressing reminders. One thing is apparent—the larger an institution grows, the less responsive it becomes to its reason for being established. Why then would we want to begin still another institution called day-care or preschool?

If we aren't more mindful of what we are doing, we'll wind up institutionalizing all age groups. We'll place all the old people in one institution and all the children in another. If we have time, we can visit them now and then. I'm not one to cry "future shock," but we must alter our course and priorities for we are already coming dangerously close to that situation.

If we choose to rear our children in communal institutions we can, of course, build the buildings and hire the personnel to organize their activities and stand guard. But it would be difficult to tell if we are guarding the children from the world or the world from the children.

The Russians have been doing this for years. In the article "Who Raises Russia's Children?" Susan Jacoby reports that nearly 80 percent of the Russian women between the ages of twenty and fifty-five are employed outside their homes. The Soviet government favors communal child rearing, "for it encourages personality formation in conformity with the collectivist ideals the state wishes to instill in all its citizens."[2]

"From the very beginning stress is placed on teaching children to share and to engage in joint activity," write Urie Bronfenbrenner and John C. Condry, Jr., in their book *Two Worlds of Childhood: U.S. and U.S.S.R.* "Frequent reference is made to common ownership: *'Moe eto nashe; nashe moe'* [mine is ours; ours is mine.] Consequently, ". . . Soviet children, in the process of growing up, are confronted with fewer divergent views both within and outside the family and, . . . conform more completely to a more homogeneous set of standards."[3]

Since the ping-pong team and former President Nixon

visited China, we have seen a rash of television documentaries showing the communal child rearing institutions there. We see that the children are well trained and function as little soldiers. It works. There is little doubt that children can be trained en masse. But is that what we want for our children? Do we want them all to dress alike and think alike? Would we so mindlessly give away our children's chances to be individuals? One would hope not.

The best chance a child has to become an individual—unique and innovative—is held within the decisions of his parents. The longer he is in their care, the better are his chances to be both individualistic and creative. If we institutionalize our children, we will be rapidly transformed into a whole nation of institutionalized people.

The *CBS News* documentary, "The I.Q. Myth," reported that one of the main reasons for the failure of *Head Start* programs is that children were taught without their mothers. The children were slow to learn and their retention was very low. Yet, during recent federally funded pilot programs in Long Island, New York, where materials and instructions were given to mothers of culturally disadvantaged two-year-olds so they could teach their children at home, Dr. Phyllis Levenstein reported that the children learned very quickly, their retention capacities were quite high, and I.Q. tests showed an average gain of fifteen points, which once again shows that I.Q. scores are not static and unchangeable.[4]

Since these programs have been in effect for over five years, the first children involved in them are now attending grade school, and through subsequent testing, it has been confirmed that those I.Q. points gained have not decreased.

In other words, they have found what Glenn Doman realized twenty-five years ago. And Shinishi Suzuki. And Claire Timmermans. And what most grandmothers have been saying for centuries. *Children should be with their mothers. They learn better when they are with their mothers.*

These conclusions shouldn't come as a surprise to us. There have been numerous studies clearly establishing the fact that institutionalized children do not develop and progress as quickly or as well as do children in a home environment.

Proponents of day-care centers and preschools will then argue that we must build better institutions. One would expect such shallow rebuttals from them. Building better institutions would be like searching for a cure for some dread disease rather than seeking a way of preventing it. The goals are confused. Isn't it obvious that if children learn better in home environments that the proper goal would be to improve our home environments rather than try to develop substitutes? The goal should be to attempt to provide ways to keep children with their mothers and to encourage their mothers to teach them. That's the proper goal!

Expecting such a goal to be initiated by governmental officials or by the school systems in this country, would require us to transcend to a state of euphoric delusions. We might just as well wait for a proclamation from the Wizard of Oz. Such a goal must be set forth by parents. If they do not, they will see bureaucratic kingdoms of day-care centers and preschools spread throughout the land in cancerous proportions. If parents do not set goals and demand that those standards be reached, then perhaps they deserve no better than they will get.

Perhaps the most baffling and the most disappointing movements toward the establishment of day-care centers is occurring in churches. For years they have been the last bastions championing family unity. But today, one rarely passes a church that doesn't have a sign on the front lawn announcing day-care or preschool facilities. It seems that they too have succumbed to the pressures of social reform.

Make Way for School-School

In the not too distant future, I think there will be still another type of day-care initiated in this country. But it won't be called day-care or preschool. I'm sure that it will be given a glorious title that is both psychologically pleasing to parents and professionally rewarding to the educators, but whatever it is called, it will be a school-school.

Someday—and that day may not be faraway—some self-professed prophet of the National Teacher's Association is going to ascend a mountain and return with a set of xeroxed tablets, announcing that he or she has just had a revelation —that he or she has become aware that four-year-olds can learn faster than five-year-olds, and that three-year-olds can learn faster than four-year-olds, and so on. Therefore, this self-professed prophet will declare, "Children should start to school at earlier ages." It's going to happen! It's going to happen! It's going to happen!

With visions of newly constructed classrooms and more jobs for professional teachers, the spokesmen for teachers' unions will totally disregard the importance of the mother-child relationship, and the fact that mothers are marvelous teachers. They will claim that mothers hold information from their children during those prime learning years. As evidence, they will cite that children who should know so much more, enter school knowing only their names, addresses, and phone numbers. It will be a vicious, circular kangaroo court! They will claim that all preschoolers should be able to read, solve mathematic problems, write complete sentences, and all of those skills that they, and their colleagues for decades, have sworn were harmful for parents to teach preschoolers.

If this is allowed to happen, our society will become more like Russia's and China's than we would like to admit. But I'm afraid the time is closer than we imagine. The climate is ripe. Over the last three decades mothers have become more and more desensitized to the realization of their importance, and today more and more of them have to work to either supplement their husband's income or to totally provide for their families. Public schools for younger children would provide free day-care—a seductive incentive indeed!

Those children who are neglected at home, and those who are left with unimaginative caretakers in detention warehouses called day-care centers, may very well have a better chance to develop and learn. But those who have eager, inventive, full-time mothers have much to lose, not only in quality and quantity of learning experiences, but also in the loss of loving companionship and much of their own individuality.

Initially, these schools will be available at the option of the parents. If they wish their toddlers to attend, they enroll them. If they would rather keep them at home, they can. Eventually, however, enrollment will become compulsory as we have seen the kindergarten classes become in the last two decades.

As much as I fear it will, I hope this prediction will not materialize. I hope that twenty or thirty years from now, someone holds this piece of writing in front of my face and says, "Melton, you dunce, you were wrong. It didn't happen!" And I'll say, "Thank God." I'll probably also say, "Thank mothers. They stopped it from happening!" And I would hope that this writing might have influenced their decision. If it does, that would please me very much.

If our experiences with our decaying school systems offer any prediction for the future, it is sad, indeed, that only a few of them will be excellent environments in which children can grow.

Unless a miracle occurs and adult attitudes alter 180 degrees, the first prerequisite for these schools will be that they are convenient for adults. It will be as it most often has been: If there is a decision between adult convenience or the welfare of children, adults will come first. Adults have the votes. Adults control the purse strings.

And what about the children? Their futures would be what their pasts have been. Their welfare has always been subject to the wishes and whims of adults.

It leads one to wonder if the meek will really inherit the earth.

If you are a mother who has to work for either financial or emotional reasons, be as selective as you can possibly afford.

One of the most important things for you to remember in selecting a place for your child is that no matter how good the facilities may be, or how efficient the people are who will care for your child, at very best, considering your child's well being, they are second best to you. I don't say this in an attempt to make you feel guilty. It is simply a statement of fact. If you must work and have no other choice but to leave your child in the care of others, there is no reason for feelings of guilt. However, it would be wise for you to feel concern and to be realistic.

Take all the time you can afford, and then some more, in finding the best place available. Don't let the inconvenience of a few extra blocks of driving or even walking convince you to select the nearest place to your residence. What is a daily six blocks of inconvenience in comparison with your child's welfare?

Make sure the place you select offers your child the most opportunities to learn. Be certain that the staff is doing more than merely warehousing children by the hour, and teaching them more than how to stack blocks and sing *London Bridge Is Falling Down.*

The child-teacher ratio is extremely important. If there are twenty children for each adult employed, you should realize that the individual attention your child will receive is divided by twenty. Even if it's five to one, his chances for the maximum attention and learning experiences are only twenty percent of those you could provide if you were with him. But numbers aren't the whole story. There are some teachers who, because of their unusual interest in children and their wild enthusiasm, can provide more learning experiences and individual attention for ten children than others can muster for five. Observe the enthusiasm of the teacher, and how the children respond to her.

Consider whether or not the place provides a clean, pleasant and stimulating environment for your child. Look over the equipment to see if it provides opportunities for learning experiences and creative expression. Don't be fooled by stacks of wooden blocks and racks of picture books. Attitudes and inventive activities are far more important than toys and things that help pass hours of waiting for you.

The staff should be teaching children to read, teaching them to write, teaching number concepts, geometrical shapes, and space relationships. Children should be drawing, painting, learning to use scissors, modeling clay, singing songs, and performing skits. Are there puzzles to work, and finger paint, and games being played for fun and to improve coordination? Is there a chinning bar across a doorway, and an exercise mat for tumbling?

Is the outdoor playground sufficient, both in space and equipment? Are there more than swings and teeter-totters? Perhaps a jungle gym to climb, suitable areas for Hopscotch and jumping rope, and an ample box of sand.

Talk with the teachers and inquire about their goals for the children. If they tell you that those in their charge are no more than little kids and there is not much they can do for them except give them orange juice and regular naptimes, grab your child in your arms and run, don't walk, to the nearest exit.

In making your decision, you might show this book to whoever is in charge and discuss the importance of early learning with them. If enough mothers show such concern, preschools and day-care centers can do nothing but improve.

Even though you must work, if you are an inventive mother, evening, weekends, and days off can still afford opportunities for you to share a multitude of learning experiences with your child. However, take care not to barrage him with too many things in your efforts to make up for the hours you are away from him. You should consider that after a full day's work, your energy level and your patience will not be at their best, and neither will your child's. Be certain your time together is enjoyable and filled with warmth.

While all of these considerations should be as urgent to fathers as they are to mothers, in the vast majority, it is the mother who must make such decisions. I'm not inferring that this is the way it should be, nor am I saying that in the future fathers will not take a more active role in seeking care for children. Today, however, it is still a rarity.

Once your child attends a day-care center, make periodic checks on the place. Take off from work with either a real or feigned headache and drop in at the center unannounced. You might do well to suggest that some of the other mothers do the same.

If you are a mother who doesn't work, then why would you want to put your child in such a place? There is every indication that you can teach him a great deal more on a one-to-one basis than he will learn in a room with twenty to thirty others.

Chapter 11

Unlimited Opportunities

The Choice Is Yours

Five years. Five years is all the time parents have with their children before the outsiders take over the hours of their days. Five years isn't a very long span of time. Toward the end, it seems much shorter than it does at the beginning. Hopefully, during these brief years, you have shaped your child into a laughing, loving, caring, intelligent human being.

The better you prepare your child for life experiences, the better he will meet the challenges and opportunities. If at the end of those five years he has developed into an active, inquisitive child, eager to learn, chances are he will function in school as an active, inquisitive child, eager to learn—and better still, he will function throughout life as an active and inquisitive human being.

As you are teaching your child, I recommend that from time to time you reread sections of this book. You will find during later stages that some of the ideas will become more meaningful, and some of the suggestions will take on added importance. Have other members of your family read it. Include grandparents and close friends, and all the people with whom your child has close contact. Their attitudes also affect your child.

One word of caution. Don't become a complete fanatic. A little fanaticism is all right but don't constantly talk about what you are doing and don't make your child the center of every conversation you have with friends and relatives. If you do, you'll soon bore them into open-mouthed yawns, and they'll start locking their doors when they see you coming.

Remember, teaching your child is a very natural thing

to do. It is a part of your function as a parent. While other people will be interested in what you are doing, and in your child's progress, they will not be consumed with the same intensity. When they ask questions, answer them with highlights or a brief synopsis; then *you* change the subject. It is better to leave them wanting more information than to stuff their eyes and ears with detailed reports and an itemized list of your child's latest accomplishments. Just by being near your child, they will see these accomplishments unfold.

At the same time you are teaching your child, you must maintain contact with the adult world of interests—politics, the latest books, other people's activities, and the needs of other members in your family. There will be many advantages to you as a person. While you are searching for more information for your child, you will find that you are reading more and becoming even more alert to the world around you. While you are teaching him to be creative, you will become more creative. While you are making him aware of different types of music, you are becoming more aware of forms and styles. As you take him on trips to museums and on sightseeing excursions, you become better informed about your community. You are also absorbing enormous amounts of information. In fact, the process of teaching your child may constitute one of the finest adult education courses you will ever have.

In the last two decades, we have learned some extremely important information about children. We have learned:

•The first five years are the most important years in a child's development.

•During those five years, fact for fact, a child learns 80 percent of all the information he will absorb during his entire life.

•The younger the child, the faster and easier he can learn.

•The preschooler can learn anything and everything we care to teach him.

•The mother-child relationship during those five years is vitally important to the child's development.

•Mothers are the best teachers for their young children.

•An excellent home environment can accelerate the child's abilities.

•IQ scores are not stationary and irrevocable. They can be altered and enhanced by many points.

•Talents are not inborn; they are created.

•Brighter children do not become strange and withdrawn; instead, they are more outgoing, personable, and inventive.

If you are the parents of a preschooler, how or if you utilize this information is your decision. And that is how it should be. Your children are your business. They are in your safekeeping. The decisions about children's lives should be left to the discretion of their parents. I trust parents and value their sensibilities and concern far above those of the professionals and governmental agencies.

My wife says that she would gladly give twenty years of her life if she could have the first five years of our children's lives again. She doesn't say this with false heroics or martyred sighs. At those times, I quickly remind her that we haven't done too badly considering the circumstances. During the course of the years, our brain-injured son has been transformed into a normal, active human being, and our daughter has most of the attributes parents wish for in a teenage girl.

"But, if we had known then what we know now," Nancy says, "just think how much more we could have taught them."

She is right, of course.

Hopefully, by passing on these things we have learned, they will be of benefit to you and your children.

How do you begin to teach your preschooler?

You begin by beginning. If you are by nature or by habit a listmaker then make a list of the materials you need and outline a program. However, if you are a more free-wheeling type, then free-wheel. Some mothers will initiate one program at a time. For instance, they will start a reading program and then add mathematics, painting, and so on. Other mothers will jump head on into all subjects at once. You know yourself and how you work best. Do it your way.

No matter what your approach, I strongly suggest that you print some cards and hang them on walls where you will see them everyday. In your child's room. In the kitchen. In the living room. Even in the bathroom.

Print the following statements:

MY CHILD CAN LEARN ANYTHING AND
EVERYTHING I CARE TO TEACH HIM.
MY CHILD HAS A GENIUS FOR LEARNING.
MY CHILD CAN LEARN MORE TODAY THAN HE
CAN NEXT YEAR.
MY CHILD'S BRAIN IS GROWING EVERYDAY.

And the statement Glenn Doman had printed on balloons:

COMPARED TO CHILDREN, ADULTS ARE
HOPELESSLY MENTALLY RETARDED.

Add any other statements that you have found meaningful in this book, and record any others you think of.

This is terribly important because, in the past, we have had so much negative input concerning children and their abilities. Until our new attitudes about their unlimited potentials are fully entrenched, we should constantly remind ourselves of this new awareness.

Now that you are aware of the importance of your child's early years, your days with him should take on new meaning and added urgency. His questions become vital. His activities become prime factors. He will begin to grow and learn at a faster pace because you expect him to grow and learn at a faster pace. He will begin to absorb more and better information because you are providing him with more and better information.

If you find that teaching your child and watching him grow is an exciting and exhilarating experience, then your child will love every minute of it.

If you find that you are having fun with your child, it will be obvious that your child is having fun too.

You are the key. Your attitudes and your actions create the atmosphere for his learning. You never have to pressure young children into learning. They want to learn. They love to learn. And they love having their accomplishments praised. In this respect, little children are very much like big people. They like to be respected and loved and all those nice things.

Remember, your prime goal is not to train your child to recite mathematic concepts or read lists of words. You are in the business of creating a healthy, loving, alert human being. That's a highly important business—one that comes very close to an act of God. It is both a gift and an opportunity. Treasure it. Realize its importance. You may never again have the chance to affect another person's life in such positive ways.

If your child is four years old, your time is short.

If he is three, you have only two years left.

If he is two, how fortunate you are.

If he is one, you are luckier still.

If he is a newborn, your opportunities to teach your child are unlimited!

A Note to Parents

During the last six years I have had four books published which deal with the problems of rearing children. *Todd* and *When Children Need Help* explore the problems confronting parents in obtaining educational and medical help for brain-injured children. *Burn the Schools—Save the Children* exposes the insanities of our school systems and offers ways parents can alter those systems. *Children of Dreams—Children of Hope* tells of Dr. Raymundo Veras' work with mongoloid children, and how many of them have become normal through revolutionary methods of therapy.

My wife and I have received many letters from parents. Without exception, they have been both friendly and heartwarming. And we try to answer as many as time permits. The ones saying, "Because we read your book, our child's life was saved," are among our favorites. Our other favorites read, "For the first time, Tommy can walk." And, "Angela can now see." And, "Robert can now talk." And, "Rebecca entered a regular class this week." They are lovely letters and so rewarding.

This book is not meant to be a one-way street from us to you. I hope that it will open a two-way avenue of understanding and communication. It wasn't written because I like to write. I'd rather do almost anything than face blank pages and the typewriter keys each morning. I've exiled myself in the studio and hammered out these pages because my wife and I are vitally interested in children and we happen to like parents. We would love to hear of your child's progress and/or any questions you may have. Feel free to write to us in care of David McKay Company, Inc., 750 Third Avenue, New York, New York, 10017, and your letter will be forwarded to us.

Chapter Notes

Chapter 2

1. Doman, Glenn J., *How to Teach Your Baby to Read,* Random House, New York, 1963, p. 105.
2. Ausubel, D.P., Sullivan, E.V., *Theory and Problems of Child Development,* Grune & Stratton, Inc., New York, 1970, p. 24.
3. Ibid., p. 26.
4. Ibid., p. 28.
5. Skinner, O., "7,000,000 Children Can't Be Wrong," *St. Louis Post-Dispatch,* May 12, 1971.
6. Bloom, B., quoted by Pines, M., "A Child's Mind Is Shaped Before Age 2," *Life,* December 17, 1971, p. 63.
7. Pines, M., "They Would Tailor an 'Intellectual Diet' for American Children," *St. Louis Globe-Democrat,* February 20, 1968. Adapted from Pines, M., *Revolution in Learning,* Harper & Row, New York, 1967.

Chapter 3

1. Ardrey, R., *African Genesis,* Dell Publishing Co., Inc., New York, 1961, p. 345.
2. Dart, R.A., with Craig, D., *Adventures with the Missing Link,* The Institutes Press, Philadelphia, 1967, p. 237.
3. Fay, T. (M.D.), compiled by Wolf, J.M. (Ed.D.), *Temple Fay, M.D.: Progenitor of the Doman-Delacato Treatment Procedures,* Charles C. Thomas, Springfield, Illinois, 1968, pp. 110, 111.
4. LeWinn, E.B. (B.S., M.D., F.A.C.P.), *Human Neurological Organization,* Charles C. Thomas, Springfield, Illinois, 1969, p. 11.
5. Bronowski, J., *The Ascent of Man,* Little, Brown and Company, Boston, 1973, p. 31.
6. Crossfield, S., *Human Potential,* Philadelphia, Vol. 1, No. 1, 1967, p. 59.
7. Hope, A., "The Brain," *Life,* October 1, 1971, New York, p. 45.

8. Doman, Glenn J., Parent Orientation Lecture, Philadelphia, 1965, quoted by Melton, D., *Todd,* Prentice-Hall, Englewood Cliffs, New Jersey, 1968, pp. 102, 103; paper: Dell Publishing Co., New York, 1968, pp. 75, 76.

9. Penfield, W. (M.D.), "The Uncommitted Cortex: The Child's Changing Brain," reprint, *The Atlantic,* Vol. 214, No. 1, p. 81.

10. Veras, R. (M.D.), with Melton, D., *Children of Dreams— Children of Hope,* Henry Regnery Company, Chicago, 1975, p. 137.

11. Krech, D., "In Search of the Ingram," MED. Op. Rev., 1966, Vol. 1, p. 20, quoted in LeWinn, E.B., *Human Neurological Organization,* Charles C. Thomas, Springfield, Illinois, 1969, p. 36.

Chapter 4

1. *Population and the American Future: The Report of the Commission on Population Growth and the American Future,* New American Library (Signet Books), New York, 1972, p. 127.

2. Reimer, E., *School Is Dead: Alternatives in Education,* Doubleday & Co., (Anchor Books), Garden City, New York, 1972, pp. 23, 24.

3. Doman, Glenn J., *How to Teach Your Baby to Read,* Random House, New York, 1963, p. 99.

4. Doman, Glenn J., Parent Orientation Lecture, The Institutes for the Achievement of Human Potential, Philadelphia, 1960.

5. Doman, Glenn J., foreword to Hughes, F., *Reading & Writing Before School,* Jonathan Cape, London, 1971, p. 7.

6. Doman, Glenn J., *How to Teach Your Baby to Read,* Random House, New York, 1963, pp. 82, 83, 84.

7. Carter, S., *Parents & Better Family Living,* "A Happy Headstart in Reading," February 1973, pp. 49, 50.

Chapter 5

1. Veras, Raymundo (M.D.) with Melton, D., *Children of Dreams—Children of Hope,* Henry Regnery Co., Chicago, 1975, p. 177.

2. Rollin, Betty, "Motherhood: Who Needs It?" *Look,* September 22, 1970, pp. 15, 16, 17.

3. *Ladies' Home Journal,* "America Writes," August 1975, p. 62.

4. Kagan, J., "His Struggle for Identity," *Saturday Review,* December 7, 1968, p. 80.

5. Silverman, C.E., *Crisis in the Classroom,* Vintage Books, New York, 1971, p. 237.

6. Cadden, V., " 'Yes' to Love and Joyful Faces," *Life,* December 17, 1971, p. 71.

7. Brazelton, T.B. (M.D.), with Main, M., "Are There Too Many Sights and Sounds in Your Baby's World?" *Redbook,* September 1971, p. 151.

8. Bronfenbrenner, U., with Condry, J.C., Jr., *Two Worlds of Childhood: U.S. and U.S.S.R.,* Pocket Books, New York, 1973, pp. 75, 76.

Chapter 6

1. Fine, B., *The Modern Family Guide to Education,* Doubleday & Co., Garden City, New York, 1962, p. 277.

2. "The Power of Positive Thinking," *Family Circle,* March 1970, pp. 32, 33.

3. Arnold, A., "Do I.Q. Tests Measure Ability of Your Child?" *St. Louis Globe-Democrat,* April 12, 1973.

4. Felix, R., quoted by Fine, B., *The Modern Family Guide to Education,* Doubleday & Co., Garden City, New York, 1962, p. 278.

5. "The I.Q. Myth," *CBS Television,* July 8, 1975.

6. Fine, B., "U.S. Gifted Children Are Neglected," *The New York Times,* May 30, 1968.

7. Valentine, C.W., "Genius," *Los Angeles Herald-Examiner,* September 1, 1968, p. 13.

8. Walters, C. Etta, "Gifted Ability Is Shown Early," *Tallahassee, Florida Democrat,* June 30, 1968.

9. Fleming, Thomas J. and Alice, "The Achievers Usually Have Skilled Parents," *Kansas City Star,* May 20, 1970, p. 2E.

Chapter 7

1. Harrison, Jay S., *Human Potential,* Philadelphia, Vol. 1. No. 1, 1967, (inside cover).

2. Laird, J.E., "Creativity: Your Greatest Gift to Your Child," *Let's Live,* September 1971, pp. 26C, 33C.

3. Fleming, Thomas J. and Alice, "Develop Your Child's Creativity," *St. Louis Globe-Democrat,* May 9, 1970.

4. Ibid.

Chapter 8

1. Fay, T. (M.D.), compiled by Wolf, J.M. (Ed.D.), *Temple Fay, M.D.: Progenitor of the Doman-Delacato Treatment Procedures,* Charles C. Thomas, Springfield, Illinois, 1968, pp. 130, 131.
2. Erhart, M., R.S.C.J., "Early Learning," *St. Louis Globe-Democrat,* June 4, 1971.
3. Kerr, G., Parent Orientation Lecture, The Institutes for the Achievement of Human Potential, Philadelphia, 1973.
4. *The Doman-Delacato Developmental Profile:* Doman, Glenn, J., The Institutes for the Achievement of Human Potential, Philadelphia, 1962, modified 1964, 1971.

Chapter 9

1. Holt, J., *How Children Learn,* Dell Publishing Co., New York, 1970, p. 153.
2. Kerr, G., Parent Orientation Lecture, The Institutes for the Achievement of Human Potential, Philadelphia, 1973.
3. Gibran, K., *The Prophet,* Alfred A. Knopf, New York, 1923, 1951, p. 18.

Chapter 10

1. Nimnicht. G., quoted by Hoffman, B.H., "Do You Know How to Play with Your Child?" *Woman's Day,* August 1972, p. 46.
2. Jacoby, S., "Who Raises Russia's Children?" *Saturday Review,* August 21, 1971.
3. Bronfenbrenner, U., with Condry, J.C., Jr., *Two Worlds of Childhood: U.S. and U.S.S.R.,* Pocket Books, New York, 1973, pp. 17, 85.
4. "The I.Q. Myth," *CBS Television,* July 8, 1975.

Index